DROPPING YOUR GUARD
The Value of Open Relationships

BIBLE STUDY GUIDE

From the Bible-teaching ministry of

Charles R. Swindoll

INSIGHT FOR LIVING

These studies are based on the outlines of sermons delivered by Charles R. Swindoll. Chuck is a graduate of Dallas Theological Seminary and has served in pastorates for over twenty-three years, including churches in Texas, New England, and California. Since 1971 he has served as senior pastor of the First Evangelical Free Church of Fullerton, California. Chuck's radio program, "Insight for Living," began in 1979. In addition to his church and radio ministries, Chuck has authored twenty books and numerous booklets on a variety of subjects.

Chuck's outlines are expanded from the sermon transcripts, and the text is coauthored by Bill Watkins, a graduate of California State University at Fresno and Dallas Theological Seminary. The Living Insights are written by Bill Butterworth, a graduate of Florida Bible College, Dallas Theological Seminary, and Florida Atlantic University. Bill Watkins is presently the director of educational products, and Bill Butterworth is currently the director of counseling ministries at Insight for Living.

Editor in Chief:	Cynthia Swindoll
Coauthor of Text:	Bill Watkins
Author of Living Insights:	Bill Butterworth
Editorial Assistant:	Julie Martin
Copy Supervisor:	Wendy Jones
Copy Assistants:	Glenda Gardner and Jane Gillis
Director, Communications Division:	Carla Beck
Project Supervisor:	Nina Paris
Art Director:	Ed Kesterson
Production Artist:	Becky Englund
Typographers:	Bob Haskins and Debbie Krumland
Cover:	Paul Lewis
Production Supervisor:	Deedee Snyder
Printer:	Frye and Smith

Unless otherwise identified, all Scripture references are from the *New American Standard Bible,* © The Lockman Foundation 1960, 1962, 1963, 1968, 1971, 1972, 1973, 1975, 1977. Used by permission.

ISBN 0-8499-82-103

Ordering Information

An album that contains twelve messages on six cassettes and corresponds to this study guide may be purchased through Insight for Living, Post Office Box 4444, Fullerton, California 92634. For ordering information and a current catalog, please write our offices or call (714) 870-9161.

Canadian residents may obtain a catalog and ordering information through Insight for Living Ministries, Post Office Box 2510, Vancouver, British Columbia, Canada V6B 3W7, (604) 272-5811. Overseas residents should direct their correspondence to our Fullerton office.

If you wish to order by Visa or MasterCard, you are welcome to use our toll-free number, (800) 772-8888, Monday through Friday between the hours of 8:30 A.M. and 4:00 P.M., Pacific time. This number may be used anywhere in the continental United States excluding Alaska, California, and Hawaii. Orders from those areas can be made by calling our general office number, (714) 870-9161.

Table of Contents

Loosening the Mask: How It All Began[1] 1

Digging Deeper, Risking Change (Part One) 6

Digging Deeper, Risking Change (Part Two) 12

Getting Closer, Growing Stronger 18

Operation Assimilation 23

United and Invincible 31

When the Fellowship Breaks Down 36

Authentic Love 43

Needed: Shelter for Storm Victims 50

Some Things Have Gotta Go! 56

Choose for Yourself 63

The Necessity of Accountability 66

A Hope Transplant: The Essential Operation[2] 71

1. The lesson "Loosening the Mask: How It All Began" is for the first chapter of the book *Dropping Your Guard* (Waco, Tex.: Word Books, 1983). There is no cassette tape that corresponds to this chapter.

2. The cassette message that corresponds to this chapter was formerly titled "Churches of Hope."

Dropping Your Guard

When I reached my tenth anniversary as the senior pastor of our church in Fullerton, California, I found myself doing some serious thinking about where we had been, where we were, and where we were going. As a result of those days and weeks of evaluation, God led me to address some specific issues: church growth; honest, unguarded relationships; the value of involvement in each other's lives; and accountability within the Body of Christ. At that time, I had no plans for developing those messages into an expository series . . . to say nothing of a book!

As one message led to another, however, it became obvious that the truths I was presenting to our local congregation were relevant and applicable for churches all around the world. What I originally presented under the title Congregational Relationships *grew into a full series and then a book, both with an entirely new title—*Dropping Your Guard.

We have attempted to provide a study guide that will deepen your understanding of the taped messages as well as each chapter of the book. We hope you will find it helpful as you think through the material on your own.

My desire is that our Lord will open your eyes to the value of authentic relationships and that His Spirit will free you to be vulnerable as you drop your guard with others in the family of God. I can assure you, the result is worth the effort.

Chuck Swindoll

Putting Truth into Action

Knowledge apart from application falls short of God's desire for His children. Knowledge must result in change and growth. Consequently, we have constructed this Bible study guide with these purposes in mind: (1) to stimulate discovery, (2) to increase understanding, and (3) to encourage application.

At the end of each lesson is a section called **Living Insights.** *There you'll be given assistance in further Bible study, thoughtful interaction, and personal appropriation. This is the place where the lesson is fitted with shoe leather for your walk through the varied experiences of life.*

In wrapping up some lessons, you'll find a unit called **Digging Deeper.** *It will provide you with essential information and list helpful resource materials so that you can probe further into some of the issues raised in those studies.*

It's our hope that you'll discover numerous ways to use this tool. Some useful avenues we would suggest are personal meditation, joint discovery, and discussion with your spouse, family, work associates, friends, or neighbors. The study guide is also practical for church classes and, of course, as a study aid for the "Insight for Living" radio broadcast. The individual studies can usually be completed in thirty minutes. However, some are more open-ended and could be expanded for greater depth. Their use is flexible!

In order to derive the greatest benefit from this process, we suggest that you record your responses to the lessons in a notebook where writing space is plentiful. In view of the kinds of questions asked, your notebook may become a journal filled with your many discoveries and commitments. We anticipate that you will find yourself returning to it periodically for review and encouragement.

Bill Watkins
Coauthor of Text

Bill Butterworth
Author of Living Insights

DROPPING YOUR GUARD

The Value of Open Relationships

Loosening the Mask:
How It All Began
Acts 2, 4; Ecclesiastes 4

Full self-disclosure is something we tend to avoid at all costs. In fact, we are prone to keep people out of our private worlds by wearing masks—not physical masks, but psychological ones. Some of us wear an "I'm tough" mask so that others won't see how weak and frightened we are. Many of us display an "I'm holy" mask, which hides our struggle with temptation and sin. The "I can handle anything" mask is another one that we commonly put on. Behind it, we may feel bewildered and hurt, but this mask makes these emotions practically undetectable by others. Are these cover-up games worth playing? Certainly not. How could a life characterized by phoniness, loneliness, and slavery to a lie ever compare to one marked by honesty, companionship, and freedom to live the truth? The latter lifestyle is the one God wants us to have; it is the one that will bring us the greatest joy. So let's commit ourselves to putting away our masks as we learn the challenges and rewards of relating to others in an unguarded way.

I. Genuine Concerns about Growth
When surveying the situations in which dropping our guard can be difficult, we discover that one example quickly rises to the top of the list: a church experiencing rapid growth in attendance. Where else is it as easy to become a face in the crowd rather than a part of the action . . . a needy loner rather than a satisfied participant in ministry? The difficulties a large church poses to spiritual growth and the development of personal relationships have caused some people to conclude that only small churches are effective in ministry. But is this conclusion warranted? Is it possible to be large in number and still deep in the things that matter?

II. Hearing God's Appraisal
Turning to Scripture, we find ample evidence to support the claim that a large body of people *can* grow deep relationally and spiritually.

The lesson "Loosening the Mask: How It All Began" is for chapter 1 of the book *Dropping Your Guard* (Waco, Tex.: Word Books, 1983). There is no cassette tape that corresponds to this chapter.

For example, in Acts, Luke makes these observations about the quickly increasing membership of the Jerusalem church:

So then, those who had received [Peter's] word were baptized; and there were added that day about three thousand souls. And they were continually devoting themselves to the apostles' teaching and to fellowship, to the breaking of bread and to prayer. And everyone kept feeling a sense of awe; and many wonders and signs were taking place through the apostles. And all those who had believed were together, and had all things in common; and they began selling their property and possessions, and were sharing them with all, as anyone might have need. And day by day continuing with one mind in the temple, and breaking bread from house to house, they were taking their meals together with gladness and sincerity of heart, praising God, and having favor with all the people. And the Lord was adding to their number day by day those who were being saved. (Acts 2:41–47)

And the congregation of those who believed were of one heart and soul; and not one of them claimed that anything belonging to him was his own; but all things were common property to them. And with great power the apostles were giving witness to the resurrection of the Lord Jesus, and abundant grace was upon them all. For there was not a needy person among them, for all who were owners of land or houses would sell them and bring the proceeds of the sales, and lay them at the apostles' feet; and they would be distributed to each, as any had need. (4:32–35)

This was definitely a dynamic and caring group of people. Obviously, size did not hinder their ability to learn God's Word, their commitment to meet one another's needs, or their choice to be open and honest with each other.

III. Considering Some Crucial Issues

The practice of the New Testament Church builds on a foundational Old Testament truth: *God created us with a need and desire for companionship* (Gen. 2:18–25). We cannot live full, rich lives unless we share ourselves with other people. That is one reason the Bible often extols the benefits of developing healthy relationships. Notice these comments from Solomon's journal, Ecclesiastes:

Two are better than one because they have a good return for their labor. For if either of them falls, the one will lift up his companion. But woe to the one who falls when there is not another to lift him up. Furthermore, if two lie down together they keep warm, but how can one be

2

warm alone? And if one can overpower him who is alone, two can resist him. A cord of three strands is not quickly torn apart. (4:9–12)

As we reflect on this passage in relationship to a church assembly, we can see that it raises at least three issues that should be seriously considered.

A. The unhealthy consequences of isolationism. Before we can become convinced of the value of involvement in others' lives, we must come to terms with the consequences of isolationism. In our day, many uphold selfishness as a virtue and a benefit. For example, humanistic philosopher Ayn Rand has expounded and defended this thesis in a number of her books.[1] In one of them she says, "Man—every man—is an end in himself, he exists for his own sake, and the achievement of his own happiness is his highest moral purpose."[2] She even has the hero in her novel *Atlas Shrugged* raise the individual to the level of deity: "And now I see the face of god, and I raise this god over the earth, this god whom men have sought since men came into being, this god who will grant them joy and peace and pride. This god, this one word: I."[3] Contrary to the claims of the advocates of individualism and self-centeredness stands the Word of our Creator, the Lord God. And He, who knows us better than we know ourselves, declares that an isolationist mentality can lead to at least four detrimental consequences. First, it can cause us to reap less profit from the work we perform (v. 9). Second, it fails to give us the support we need to get up and move on after a serious failure or defeat (v. 10). Third, it forces us to confront potentially threatening situations with nothing but our own inadequate resources (v. 11). And fourth, isolationism makes it practically impossible for us to overcome dangers that only two or more people can sufficiently handle (v. 12).

B. The essential benefits of relationships. Returning once again to Solomon's words, we discover four significant benefits for those who pull together rather than remain separate:
1. Through mutual effort they have a good return for their labor (v. 9).
2. Through mutual support they lift each other up (v. 10).
3. Through mutual encouragement they face threatening times (v. 11).
4. Through mutual strength they resist attacks (v. 12).

---

1. Ayn Rand's egocentric philosophy is explained and evaluated in Norman L. Geisler's book *Is Man the Measure? An Evaluation of Contemporary Humanism* (Grand Rapids, Mich.: Baker Book House, 1983), chap. 6.

2. Ayn Rand, *For the New Intellectual* (New York: Signet, 1961), as quoted by Geisler in *Is Man the Measure?*, p. 70.

3. Ayn Rand, *Atlas Shrugged,* as quoted by Geisler in *Is Man the Measure?*, p. 70.

In short, it is only when we share life's experiences that we are able to enjoy or endure them to the greatest degree. The early Christians recognized this truth and sought to apply it from the time of their initiation into the Body of Christ. They strove for authentic *koinōnía*—that is, the kind of fellowship that is marked by a vulnerable and loving involvement in the lives of fellow believers.[4] As a result, they grew personally, corporately, and evangelistically. Indeed, they turned the ancient world upside down for Christ. How much we can gain if we will only choose to remove our masks!

C. The absolute necessity of assimilation. Given the consequences of isolationism and the benefits of relationships, at least one question remains: How can a growing church continue to effectively move its people from the spectators' stands to the playing field of authentic Christianity? The answer is by maintaining a firm commitment to assimilation—that is, by becoming absorbed in the life of the Body of Christ as participants who relate to, share with, and care for others in the Church. Until we embrace this commitment on both a personal and a congregational level, it is doubtful that we will reach the spiritual maturity God longs for us to achieve while on earth. However, if we are serious about growing up in Christ, we will open ourselves up to what God has to say about dropping our guard and cultivating loving relationships with others.

Living Insights

Study One

Have you ever thought about the enormous crowd Moses had to contend with during Israel's wilderness wanderings? Hundreds of thousands of Hebrews! If you happen to be involved in a large group, you know it's easy to feel lost and alone in a crowd. Even in churches, individuals and their needs can be overlooked. But it doesn't have to be that way. It's possible to be large in number and strong in personal involvement. Size and depth *can* coexist.

- A good example of size and depth coexisting is found in Acts. The early Church grew numerically as well as relationally. Copy the following chart into your notebook. As you read the passages listed, look for the benefits of a relationship-oriented lifestyle and contrast them with what you know to be the consequences of isolationism.

4. A full discussion of Christian fellowship can be found in the study guide titled *Koinōnía: Authentic Fellowship,* ed. Bill Watkins, from the Bible-teaching ministry of Charles R. Swindoll (Fullerton, Calif.: Insight for Living, 1985).

4

After recording your findings, think of some ways you can encourage the development of relationships in your church.

Growth: Size and Depth		
References in Acts	Benefits of Relationships	Consequences of Isolationism
2:42–45		
4:32–35		
5:12–16		
8:4–8		

 Living Insights

Are you part of a large church assembly or a small one? Whichever answer you give, the issues of isolationism, relational development, and assimilation are paramount. The questions given below are designed to help you think through these important subjects on a personal level.

—In what ways could you find isolation to be unhealthy for you?

—What are some benefits you've experienced from being involved in relationships?

—Is assimilation important to you? Why or why not?

Digging Deeper, Risking Change
(Part One)
Exodus 13–14, Numbers 11

Most of us resist change with all our might. Once we become comfortable in the way we do things, we tend to settle down and fossilize in our rut. But what if our situation were to become miserable? Then would we be willing to give up the familiar and move on to personally uncharted territory? One would think so, but it is rarely the case. Being creatures of habit, many of us would rather put up with today's familiar unhappiness than embark on tomorrow's uncertain adventure. What is true of us as individuals is also true of the churches we attend; local assemblies often resist change as ardently as individuals do. Given this tendency, how can we break out of our rut? Sometimes, the Lord waits for us to alter our own routines. Other times, however, He steps in and shakes things up. But regardless of how change occurs in our lives, two things need to be grasped: If we are going to drop our guard and become vulnerable people, we must be willing to risk change. And when change occurs, we must be prepared to resist the temptations that can persuade us to retreat to the familiar. Let's consider these foundational issues in light of some of Israel's past experiences. Although our study will take two lessons to complete, we will quickly see how much we and the early Hebrews have in common.

I. Tests That Tempt Us to Retreat

Under the leadership of a man named Joseph, the Hebrews were transported from Canaan to Egypt, where they multiplied in population and grew in prosperity (Gen. 41:38–Exod. 1:7). Sometime after Joseph's death, an Egyptian monarch initiated a policy that enslaved the Hebrews, causing them tremendous pain and anguish (Exod. 1:8–22). It was in this context of bondage that God called Moses to lead His people out of Egypt (3:1–4:17). The Lord's plan for deliverance included a steady stream of miraculous judgments on the Egyptians and an incredible escape through the Red Sea for the Israelites (7:1–14:31). God even supplied all the Hebrews' needs while leading them to the Promised Land. But the Israelites struggled with their new life of freedom—one that was guided by God's gracious hand. Rather than appreciating all the Lord was doing for them, they kept giving in to the temptation to retreat to their familiar lifestyle of bondage (see Num. 14:1–4). Like us, they kept resisting God's attempts to strip them of their independence so that they would place their full trust in Him. God designed several tests to provide opportunities for the Israelites to move into a faith-oriented lifestyle. Five of these were: unfamiliar surprises, unwanted fears, unpleasant adversities, unfair

In the book this message comprises the first part of chapter 2, pp. 28–35.

accusations, and unexpected resistance. Let's look at the first three tests in this lesson. We will cover the last two in the next study.

A. Unfamiliar surprises. Through Moses, the Lord promised the Israelites that He would take them to Canaan—" 'a land flowing with milk and honey' " (Exod. 13:5b). However, He did not tell them in advance how He was going to get them there. The most direct route from Egypt to Canaan was through the land of Philistia. But God had a different way in mind. He knew that the seemingly easy path had a serious danger that could have caused the Hebrews to return to Egypt out of fear (v. 17b). "Hence God led the people around by the way of the wilderness to the Red Sea" (v. 18a). From the perspective of the Israelites, it must have seemed illogical for God to have chosen this route. After all, the wilderness was dry, rocky, and dotted with mountains. How could such a barren land possibly provide sustenance for over two million Hebrew travelers?[1] But the Lord chose the path that was best for His people, and He comforted them by displaying His guiding presence through "a pillar of cloud by day" and "a pillar of fire by night" (v. 21).

A Practical Word

God's leading frequently does not fit our expectations. Although this may cause us some confusion and frustration, we should never forget that He always has our best interest in mind. Realizing this will help us handle His surprises with less fear and greater trust.

B. Unwanted fears. God led the Israelites to the western bank of the Red Sea and had them set up camp (14:1–2). While the people were resting, Pharaoh gathered together his charioteers and horsemen and took out after the Hebrews (vv. 5–9).

> And as Pharaoh drew near, the sons of Israel looked, and behold, the Egyptians were marching after them, and they became very frightened; so the sons of Israel cried out to the Lord. Then they said to Moses, "Is it because there were no graves in Egypt that you have taken us away to die in the wilderness? Why have you dealt with us in this way, bringing us out of Egypt? Is this not the word that we spoke to you in Egypt, saying, 'Leave us alone that we may serve the Egyptians'? For it would have been better for us to serve the Egyptians than to die in the wilderness." (vv. 10–12)

1. Old Testament scholar John J. Davis supplies the reasoning behind the conclusion that over two million people were involved in the Exodus. See his book *Moses and the Gods of Egypt: Studies in the Book of Exodus* (Grand Rapids, Mich.: Baker Book House, 1971), p. 146.

From a geographical standpoint, the panic of the Hebrews is understandable. With mountains to the north, desert to the south, the Red Sea in front of them, and the Egyptian military behind them, they were boxed in. But instead of trusting in God's promise to deliver them safely to Canaan, they allowed fear to squelch their faith and turn them against Moses, the Lord's chosen leader. Certainly, the people wanted to be delivered from bondage and blessed with freedom. But when the unexpected happened and their security was threatened, the familiar life of a slave began to look awfully good. Moses tried to calm their fear, exhorting them to anticipate God's deliverance (vv. 13–14). Then the Lord commanded Moses to order the people to move toward the Red Sea (v. 15). Once the Hebrews were ready, Moses obeyed God's instructions to raise his staff over the water (vv. 16, 21a). What the people witnessed was incredible! From shore to shore, a pathway was miraculously etched through the sea. And as a strong east wind held back the water, it also dried out the once soaked ground (v. 21b). So on dry land, the Israelites passed through the midst of the sea to safety on the easternmost shore (v. 22). The Egyptians, however, were not about to give up without a fight. They continued to pursue the Hebrews through the passageway in the sea. As they did, God "caused their chariot wheels to swerve, and He made them drive with difficulty" (v. 25a). This prompted the Egyptians to begin retreating to the western shore. But before they could reach it, the Lord used Moses to cause the walls of water to collapse and drown them (vv. 26–28). "Thus the Lord saved Israel . . . from the hand of the Egyptians, and Israel saw the Egyptians dead on the seashore. And when Israel saw the great power which the Lord had used against the Egyptians, the people feared the Lord, and they believed in the Lord and in His servant Moses" (vv. 30–31).

A Practical Word

Like the Israelites, we want everything to be familiar and safe. But God often places us in situations where our security is threatened and the outcome seems unsure. When we face these tests, we may want to complain and retreat as the Hebrews did. However, the Lord's desire is that we rely on His ability and willingness to help us pass through these trials. Just as Moses obediently followed God's lead without doubting, so we should continue to trust in the Lord even when our circumstances appear hopeless and frightening.

C. Unpleasant adversities. One would think that the Israelites' miraculous exodus from Egypt would have solidified their trust in God. But it did not take long for their faith and enthusiasm to wane. While guiding the Hebrews through the desert regions of the Sinai Peninsula, the Lord supplied a breadlike substance called manna for them to eat (16:8–35). And though they never went hungry, the Israelites griped about the lack of variety in their diet: " 'Who will give us meat to eat? We remember the fish which we used to eat free in Egypt, the cucumbers and the melons and the leeks and the onions and the garlic, but now our appetite is gone. There is nothing at all to look at except this manna' " (Num. 11:4b–6). They had grown so accustomed to Egyptian cuisine that they came to regard God's gracious provision with contempt. Rather than accepting some unpleasant adversities on their journey to the Promised Land, they expected their trip to be problem-free. Indeed, their demands were so great that Moses compared them to a nursing infant and himself to their nurse (v. 12).

A Practical Word

What manna was to the Hebrews, people sometimes are to us. Frequently, God brings individuals into our lives who need our care and concern. At first, helping them is a joyful and rewarding experience. After a time, however, the task can become burdensome, and our appetite for loving involvement in the lives of others may diminish. Eventually, we may even find ourselves longing for the days when we were not so sought after, forgetting how lonely and useless we often felt during those times. We can avoid falling into that trap by remembering this truth: A heavenly appetite is required to enjoy heavenly food. We will not appreciate the blessings and responsibilities God gives us until we come to desire Him and His will more than anything else on earth.

II. A Thought That Prods Us to Press On

Despite the desire we may have to retreat to familiar territory when trials and tests come our way, we need to press forward and trust in God. For by doing this, we will derive one of the greatest benefits God's tests can bring—spiritual maturity. As the Apostle James writes in his epistle, "Consider it all joy, my brethren, when you encounter various trials, knowing that the testing of your faith produces endurance. And let endurance have its perfect result, that you may be perfect and complete, lacking in nothing" (James 1:2–4).

The path toward spiritual maturity may be risky, threatening, and arduous at times. But if we really want to deepen our faith and our relationships with others, we will choose to travel this road regardless of what comes our way. Are you willing to accept the challenge?

 Living Insights

Study One ━━━━━━━━━━━━━━━━━━━━━━━━━━━━━━━━━━━━━━━

There is an amazing analogy between the Hebrews in the days of Moses and twentieth-century Christians. Have you ever tried to put yourself in the sandals of those Hebrews when they came to the Red Sea?

• Turn in your Bible to Exodus 13. Begin in verse 17 and read through the end of chapter 14. Try to retell the story in your own words. Relate the story as if you were one of the people following Moses out of Egypt. You may want to write out your version or say it aloud. However you choose to do it, make the story alive, relevant, and personally meaningful.

 Living Insights

Study Two ━━━━━━━━━━━━━━━━━━━━━━━━━━━━━━━━━━━━━━━

Change—a word that excites some people and scares others. What is your attitude toward change? Attempt to sum up your feelings on a page from your notebook.

My Attitude toward Change

Digging Deeper, Risking Change
(Part Two)
Exodus 13–14, Numbers 11–14

When we are faced with the choice between embracing an uncertain tomorrow or returning to a secure yesterday, many of us would probably choose to go back to the familiar and the safe. Indeed, no matter how boring or painful our past may have been, we tend to gravitate toward it rather than trusting in God to guide us throughout our future. As we saw in our last lesson, the Israelites were no different than we are. God repeatedly manifested His presence to them and abundantly met their needs. His loving provisions, however, did not curb the Hebrews' resistance to change. In fact, the people became increasingly discontent and grew more determined than ever to return to the secure yet oppressive lifestyle they had experienced in Egypt. What prompted them to want to go back? And why, in spite of their desires, did they remain on the road to Canaan? What can we learn from their experience? These are the questions we will seek to answer in this lesson.

I. More Tests That Tempt Us to Go Back

In the last study we examined three of the trials God gave the Hebrews for their spiritual benefit—unfamiliar surprises, unwanted fears, and unpleasant adversities. We also saw how miserably the people failed each of these tests. Because of their attachment to the familiar and their unwillingness to trust God for the future, the Israelites continued to flunk the tests they were given. Two more of these trials were unfair accusations and unexpected resistance. Let's look at both of them and see how they apply to the situations in which we find ourselves.

A. Unfair accusations. During their wilderness wanderings, the Hebrews often vented their discontentment and anger on Moses. Even Aaron and Miriam, Moses' own brother and sister, struck out at him on one occasion. They came to Moses and questioned his capability as a leader because he had chosen a Cushite woman to be his wife (Num. 12:1).

A Practical Word

We who are in leadership positions will sometimes be misunderstood and unfairly accused. On some of these occasions, charges will undoubtedly be made on the basis of our personal, not professional, choices. And, unfortunately, a few unjustified criticisms may come from close friends and family members. But, regardless of who brings the complaints or why they are brought, we need to prepare ourselves for their inevitable arrival by maintaining a close walk with the Lord as Moses did (cf. vv. 3, 6–8). This approach will help us withstand false accusations with integrity and humility.

B. Unexpected resistance. After the Israelites arrived at the southern edge of Canaan, they pushed God to His limit. The purpose of their journey had been to travel from a den of slavery to a home of promise. And all along the way, the Lord had repeatedly confirmed His commitment to and care for the Hebrews, even when they were unfaithful. Given these things, one would think that the people would have finally decided to trust the Lord by the time they reached the Promised Land and heard the spies' report regarding Canaan's incredible fertility and abundance (13:25–27). Unfortunately, the Israelites also chose to listen to those spies who feared that the inhabitants of Canaan were too big and strong to be overtaken (vv. 31–33). As a consequence,

> the sons of Israel grumbled against Moses and Aaron; and the whole congregation said to them, "Would that we had died in the land of Egypt! Or would that we had died in this wilderness! And why is the Lord bringing us into this land, to fall by the sword? Our wives and our little ones will become plunder; would it not be better for us to return to Egypt?" So they said to one another, "Let us appoint a leader and return to Egypt." (14:2–4)

A Practical Word

How often have we responded to difficulties as the Hebrews did! Rather than finding strength in the Lord and pushing forward, we succumb to the fear within ourselves and seek to retreat. But there is no good reason to respond like this to the hurdles in our lives. If God tells us to move, we can be confident that He will help us overcome any barriers looming in our path. All we need to do is rely on Him and keep advancing as He directs. The rest is up to Him.

II. Barriers That Keep Us from Returning

As we reflect on how often the Israelites wanted to turn back to Egypt, we might ask, Why didn't they return? What kept them from acting on their desire to retreat? By looking back at the biblical record, we can discover five factors that provide the answer to these questions. As we examine each one, we will observe how they relate to us in our day.

A. Clear direction from above. Whenever the Hebrews felt the urge to give up and go back to Egypt, they could always look up and see that God was with them. During the daylight hours, the Lord manifested His guiding hand through a pillar of cloud. And throughout the evening, He used a pillar of fire to lead the people (Exod. 13:21–22). Indeed, God never kept the Israelites guessing, but always gave them clear direction from above. In our day, the Lord directs His people primarily through His written Word. But at certain junctures in our lives, He may guide us by other means. However He chooses to lead us, we can always find needed encouragement and confidence when we recall those times we received unmistakable direction from Him.[1] In addition, we can always take comfort in the fact that God will never abandon us. Once we become part of His forever family by placing our trust in Christ, He will always be with us, meeting our needs (Ps. 32:6–8; Isa. 41:10–13, 49:15–16; Rom. 8:31–37).

B. Incredible deliverance from danger. With the Egyptians in hot pursuit of the Hebrews, God commanded His people to march toward the Red Sea. As they obeyed, He created a way of escape for them through the waters of the sea. The Lord does the same today. He may wait until the last moment to deliver us from danger, but when He chooses to act, we need to be ready to move out in faith.

C. Timely relief from discouragement. Probably one of the most disheartening times in Moses' career came when his brother and sister challenged his leadership (Num. 12:1–2). While at such a low ebb, it would have been easy for Moses to have given them the reins and walked away for good. But Moses left his defense up to God, and the Lord stepped in and dealt with his critics in a way that upheld him as the Lord's chosen leader (vv. 5–15). When we face unjustified opposition, we too should trust God for our defense (Rom. 12:19). All He asks from us is that we remain faithful to Him, regardless of the charges we might face.

D. Internal fortification to withstand attack. On another occasion, a couple of men in the Israelites' camp began to prophesy. When Joshua heard about it, he took it as a threat to

---

1. Some helpful materials on divine guidance are these: Garry Friesen, *Decision Making and the Will of God: A Biblical Alternative to the Traditional View,* a Critical Concern Book (Portland: Multnomah Press, 1980); John MacArthur, Jr., *Found: God's Will* (Wheaton, Ill.: Victor Books, 1973); R. C. Sproul, *God's Will and the Christian* (Wheaton, Ill.: Tyndale House Publishers, 1984); Charles R. Swindoll, *God's Will: Biblical Direction for Living* (Portland: Multnomah Press, 1981); and Dallas Willard, *In Search of Guidance: Developing a Conversational Relationship with God* (Ventura, Calif.: Regal Books, 1984).

Moses' role as God's spokesman. So he advised Moses to restrain the two men (Num. 11:28). Moses, however, turned to Joshua and responded with words that conveyed a deep inner security: "'Are you jealous for my sake? Would that all the Lord's people were prophets, that the Lord would put His Spirit upon them!'" (v. 29). Moses did not fall prey to a competitive or exclusive spirit. His abiding relationship with God gave him the fortitude he needed to reject jealousy and replace it with applause. The Lord desires to strengthen us as He did Moses. But in order for Him to do so, we must commit ourselves to deepening our walk with Him.

E. **Extreme discipline from God.** After the Israelites steadfastly refused to enter the Promised Land, God kept them from returning to Egypt by taking their lives during the forty-year period in which they wandered in the deserts of the Sinai Peninsula. The only adult Hebrews who were exempt from this judgment were Caleb and Joshua—the two spies who had urged the people to take Canaan as their rightful possession. All the other adults, those twenty years of age and older, died in the barren wilderness (14:20–38). This teaches us that God is serious about His desire for us to move ahead and risk change His way. At times, we may want to return to the security of the past or do what we can to protect our space, time, prestige, and power. But we must never forget that when God decides we need to press forward, we dare not resist Him.

III. Responses That Cause Us to Go Further

How can we counteract the lure of the familiar so that we can continue moving into unfamiliar territory? The answer lies in our willingness to make three responses to God.

A. **Since it is God's desire that we demonstrate His distinctive message to the world around us, we should pray, "Lord, intensify your distinctives in me."** As He makes us into the kind of individuals He wants us to be, we will begin to have a unique impact on those around us.

B. **Since it is the uncertainty of our future that strengthens our faith, we should pray, "Lord, increase the risk."** Part of the thrill of the Christian life comes through trusting God to give us what we cannot provide for ourselves. And as we see Him come through for us, our motivation to take greater risks for Him will grow.

C. **Since God has designed each one of us to be a unique vessel of power, we should pray, "Lord, enlarge the difference I make."** By making ourselves available to God, we will open more opportunities for Him to spread the gospel message and renew His Church.

🌼 Living Insights

In our study of the Hebrews' journey to the Promised Land, we have seen five tests that tempted them to return to the land of the Pharaohs. Even though Egypt had been the scene of their slavery, the change God was bringing into their lives seemed terribly risky.

- The five tests we examined are listed in the following chart. Can you think of other individuals in Scripture that were confronted with tests similar to the ones faced by the Hebrews? After copying this chart into your notebook, locate a few other biblical stories that relate how people handled comparable trials. Then jot down some of your observations concerning the similarities and differences between the response they had to their tests and the Hebrews' response to theirs.

Tests That Tempt Us to Go Back		
Hebrews' Tests	Comparable Tests	Similarities and Differences
Unfamiliar Surprises		
Unwanted Fears		
Unpleasant Adversities		
Unfair Accusations		
Unexpected Resistance		

🌼 Living Insights

Being creatures of habit, most of us would rather have the security of yesterday than the uncertainty of tomorrow. Consequently, we often resist change even when it is in our best interest. Let's consider what we can do to lower our resistance to healthy change.

- This lesson ended with three objectives we should pray for to help prepare us for facing an uncertain future. On a page in your notebook, write out some of your thoughts regarding each of these responses to God. Your thoughts may include some questions, admissions of struggle, prayer requests, or statements of commitment. But whatever you jot down, make it personal and unguarded.

Responses That Cause Us to Go Further

Lord, intensify Your distinctives in me!

Lord, increase the risk!

Lord, enlarge the difference I make!

Getting Closer, Growing Stronger
Deuteronomy 6, Joshua 1

Few things are as contagious as spontaneous, unguarded love in action. But it cannot come alive or grow without the presence of three essential ingredients. One is *the admission of a need for other people.* As we saw in the previous lesson, self-sufficiency and isolationism are enemies we need to fight. If we are going to make it through life or be effective in ministry, we dare not try to go it alone. Another key element is *the cultivation of deep relationships.* Of course, putting this into practice takes a great deal of time and effort, but the dividends far outweigh the personal cost. Finally, there must be *a firm commitment to assimilation.* As we come to realize the tremendous value of each person in the Body of Christ, we will seek to encourage and serve them in their spiritual growth and Christian service. Although it is important for all of us to make these foundational elements a part of our lives, it is also crucial that we realize the dangers which threaten to move us away from obtaining an unguarded lifestyle. By becoming aware of these hazards, we will be less prone to fall prey to them. So let's spend some time exposing them and then close our study by focusing on the positive steps we can take to avoid these pitfalls.

I. Dangers to Avoid

After forty years of wandering in the desert regions of the Sinai Peninsula, the Israelites were finally ready to enter Canaan—the Promised Land. But Moses, the man God had used to lead them for so long, could not cross the border with them. His final outburst of anger brought a divine judgment that excluded him from entering Canaan (Num. 20:2–12).[1] So Moses sought to prepare the Hebrews to take possession of the land by giving them some God-ordained counsel. Embedded in the words he spoke are warnings against four dangers that are as pertinent to us today as they were to the Israelites so many centuries ago.

A. Falling more in love with the leader than with the Lord. Observe what Moses said:

"Now this is the commandment, the statutes and the judgments which the Lord your God has commanded me to teach you, that you might do them in the land where you are going over to possess it, so that you and your son and your grandson might fear the Lord your God, to keep all His statutes and His commandments, which I command you, all the days of your

---

1. A more complete account of Moses' struggles with anger can be found in the study guide titled *Moses: God's Man for a Crisis,* ed. Bill Watkins, from the Bible-teaching ministry of Charles R. Swindoll (Fullerton, Calif.: Insight for Living, 1985), pp. 90–93. Also provided in that study guide, on page 109, is a helpful bibliography on the subject of dealing with emotions.

life, and that your days may be prolonged.... Hear,
O Israel! The Lord is our God, the Lord is one! And
you shall love the Lord your God with all your heart
and with all your soul and with all your might."
(Deut. 6:1–5)

Moses knew that he would soon be taken away from the
Israelites and that another person would be stepping into his
shoes of leadership. Because of this, he wanted to assure the
people that although human leaders would come and go, the
Lord would always be with them, sustaining and protecting
them regardless of their circumstances. Therefore Moses called
on the Hebrews to devote themselves fully to God. By doing this,
the Israelite leader was alerting the people to the danger of
exalting an earthly authority over the heavenly One. Only the
Lord is worthy of our ultimate loyalty and deepest expressions
of love. And He alone provides the spiritual cement that binds
believers together into a unified whole. As long as we base our
conduct on these truths, we will find ourselves encouraging
teamwork, not hero worship, in the accomplishment of the tasks
of ministry.

**B. Fixing our eyes on our immediate convenience
instead of our ultimate objective.** Continuing to render
wise counsel to the Hebrews, Moses exhorted:

"And these words, which I am commanding you today,
shall be on your heart; and you shall teach them
diligently to your sons and shall talk of them when
you sit in your house and when you walk by the way
and when you lie down and when you rise up. And
you shall bind them as a sign on your hand and they
shall be as frontals on your forehead. And you shall
write them on the doorposts of your house and on
your gates." (vv. 6–9)

Moses did not want the Israelites to move into Canaan and
become spiritually lethargic. So he urged them to work hard at
making their knowledge of God and His ways the central focus
and foundation of their lives. By doing so, they would develop
a lifestyle of mutual sharing and caring—a way of life that would
help carry them through the tough times and provide them with
great delight during the periods of prosperity. Today, too many
of us are caught in the "sit, soak, and sour" syndrome. We are
prone to sacrifice our relationships with those around us and
with the Lord on the altar of convenience. What we need to do
is center our lives on God and His desires. Only then will we
find the details of both our private and public worlds beginning
to fall into place.

19

C. Assuming that size means strength. Moses realized how easy it is for people to think that great numbers and large assets equal incredible strength. So he warned the Hebrews that their ability to stay strong did not rest in their size or possessions but in the Lord (vv. 10–13). How obvious this truth seems! A family is not strong because it has many children; a city's strength does not reside in the size of its buildings or population; and a church's effectiveness in meeting people's needs is not predicated on how many members it has or on how much it receives in contributions. Rather, strength is found in God, and it is developed on a horizontal level through the giving of ourselves to others.

D. Living in the glow of yesterday instead of the challenge of tomorrow. After receiving the reigns of leadership formerly held by Moses, Joshua was given these words of instruction from the Lord:

> "Be strong and courageous, for you shall give this people possession of the land which I swore to their fathers to give them. . . . Have I not commanded you? Be strong and courageous! Do not tremble or be dismayed, for the Lord your God is with you wherever you go." (Josh. 1:6–9)

In response to this command, Joshua went to the officers of the people and said, " 'Pass through the midst of the camp and command the people, saying, "Prepare provisions for yourselves, for within three days you are to cross this Jordan, to go in to possess the land which the Lord your God is giving you, to possess it" ' " (v. 11). The Israelites were not to live in the past but were to press on to the future, for they would never receive the blessings that awaited them until they took on the challenge of conquering Canaan. The Lord exhorts us in a similar vein today. He does not want believers to remain static or to retreat. His desire is that we advance toward new horizons as He opens and leads the way.

II. Principles to Apply

Now that we are aware of these dangers, we need to consider what positive steps we can take to avoid them. The application of the following three principles will provide the direction we need.

A. To go on, we must get closer. At times, developing relationships may involve disruptions of our privacy and challenges to our patience. But these are minor inconveniences compared with the personal and corporate benefits closeness to others can bring.

B. To get closer, we must pull together. We need to rejoice in the happiness of others, feel the pain of those who hurt, and seek to help the needy. In other words, pulling together requires our unselfish participation in people's lives.

C. To pull together, we must grow deeper. As our walk with God becomes stronger, our ability to cultivate relationships with fellow Christians will heighten. And as we become more vulnerable in our relationships, we will find our unity with believers increasing. These are the challenges before us. Are you willing to meet them?

Living Insights

Study One

The instructions given in Deuteronomy 6 are directed toward two generations—parents and their children. Let's look at these exhortations more closely.

● Copy the following chart into your notebook. As you read through Deuteronomy 6:1–25, jot down your observations on both generations. Look for any similarities, differences, cause and effect relationships, and so on between the two groups.

Deuteronomy 6:1–25

First Generation—Parents		Second Generation—Children	
Observations	Verses	Observations	Verses

Continued on next page

Living Insights

In this lesson four dangers were presented that can threaten even the finest of ministries. Their entrance is subtle and without fanfare, but their eroding effect is destructive. Let's take some more time to increase our familiarity with them so that we can better avoid them.

• For each danger listed below, first give some illustrations of that particular pitfall from Scripture or secular history. Then write down any experiences that illustrate the presence and consequences of these hazards in your own life.

1. Falling more in love with the leader than with the Lord
2. Fixing our eyes on our immediate convenience instead of our ultimate objective
3. Assuming that size means strength
4. Living in the glow of yesterday instead of the challenge of tomorrow

Dangers to Avoid		
Illustrations from Scripture	Illustrations from Secular History	Illustrations from My Life
1.		
2.		
3.		
4.		

Operation Assimilation
Joshua 1:1–18

Surveying churches today, we find far more spectators of ministry than participants in ministry. Almost every congregation has a handful of believers who knock themselves out to get the work done while the vast majority sit back and observe from a distance. But this is not how the Body of Christ is supposed to function. God has designed the Church in such a way that its unity and effectiveness are dependent on the active involvement of all its members. Moreover, the effective participation of believers in Christian service requires the development of close relationships among God's people (1 Cor. 12:4–13:8). In short, the way to overcome congregational inertia is to initiate operation assimilation. Exactly what this is and how we can implement it will be our focus in this study.

I. Assimilation Defined
Before talking about assimilation, we need to understand what it means. For our purposes, *assimilation* refers to people reaching out to one another in love. If we think of it in relation to the Body of Christ, the term takes on a more specific meaning: *believers becoming absorbed in the life of the family of God as participants who relate to, share with, and care for others in the Church.* Written between the lines of this definition is the truth that assimilation does not begin corporately or happen automatically. Each of us who has accepted Christ as Savior is personally responsible to become involved in the lives of others (Matt. 25:31–46; Heb. 10:23–25, 13:1–3).

II. Assimilation Exemplified
Now that we know what assimilation means, let's look at the Hebrews and see how they worked it out in their lives. We should recall that prior to crossing Canaan's border, the Israelites were suffering extreme oppression in Egypt. Through Moses, God freed them from bondage and led them out to the desert region of the Sinai Peninsula. The Lord met their needs in spite of their complaints and unfaithfulness while they traveled from Egypt to Canaan. After reaching the Promised Land, the Israelites initiated a reconnaissance mission that ended with two of their spies calling on the people to advance and ten urging them to retreat. The Hebrews' decision to side with the majority report brought a divine judgment that kept virtually all the Israelites twenty-one years and older out of Canaan. When this generation finally died off, the remaining Hebrews accepted the challenge of conquering Canaan under a new leader, Joshua. What did they do to prepare themselves for this task? They united and began working together—put another way, they initiated operation assimilation. This is clearly brought out in the first chapter of Joshua,

where we find four things the Hebrews did that enabled them to march into Canaan as an effective military unit.

A. They relied on God for their future. Following the death of Moses, God came to Joshua and commanded him to lead the Hebrews across the Jordan River and into Canaan (Josh. 1:1–2). The Lord promised him that he and the people would be successful in their attempt to take the land (v. 5). As incredible as this plan seemed, Joshua and the Israelites placed their trust in God's ability to help them accomplish it. So, outnumbered and out-armed, they prepared for warfare (vv. 10–18). Throughout history, many individuals who have placed their faith in the all-powerful God have altered the course of entire countries and civilizations. Among this group of saints are the Apostle Paul, Augustine, Thomas Aquinas, Ulrich Zwingli, Martin Luther, John Calvin, John Knox, and John Wesley.[1] People such as these took great risks, realizing they could trust their future to the Creator, Sustainer, and Redeemer of the universe. The God they served has not changed. He still desires His people to accept humanly impossible challenges with their eyes securely fixed on Him. As they do, they will discover the God-given ability to conquer new frontiers for Christ.

B. They accepted the challenge without fear of failure. Three times the Lord told Joshua to be a strong and courageous leader (vv. 6, 7, 9). And the Hebrews, after confirming their commitment to Joshua, reiterated the charge to him to be a confident, fearless commander (v. 18). God and His people knew that the fear of failure was one of the greatest enemies which would have to be faced in the conquering of Canaan. So they united in their support of Joshua, thereby enabling him to lead the invasion with resolute boldness and tenacity. With God on our side, we can have confidence that there are no hopeless situations, only people who have grown hopeless about them. What may appear to us as unmeetable challenges or unsolvable problems are really exciting opportunities for us to lock arms with God and advance with Him into a life of adventure and reward.

---

1. Excellent introductions to many Christians who have stood out in church history are provided in these materials: *Heritage of Freedom,* A Lion Book (Belleville, Mich.: Lion Publishing Corp., 1984); *Faith's Heroes: A Fresh Look at Ten Great Christians,* by Sherwood Eliot Wirt (Westchester, Ill.: Cornerstone Books, 1979); *The Wycliffe Biographical Dictionary of the Church,* by Elgin Moyer, rev. ed. (Chicago: Moody Press, 1982); *A Dictionary of Women in Church History,* by Mary L. Hammack (Chicago: Moody Press, 1984); *Eerdmans' Handbook to Christianity in America* (Grand Rapids, Mich.: William B. Eerdmans Publishing Co., 1983); *The New International Dictionary of the Christian Church,* rev. ed. (Grand Rapids, Mich.: Zondervan Publishing House, 1978); and *Evangelical Dictionary of Theology,* ed. Walter A. Elwell (Grand Rapids, Mich.: Baker Book House, 1984).

C. They ignored their differences and closed ranks in unity. After receiving marching orders from the Lord, Joshua commanded the officers under him to order the people to prepare for action (vv. 10–11). Then Joshua instructed the Hebrews to lay aside tribal distinctions and to bind together in their fight to possess the Promised Land (vv. 12–15). When the Israelites heard Joshua's game plan, they accepted it as God's strategy for victory and rallied around it (vv. 16–18). As a united people with a single objective, they stood as a formidable and fearsome force. Several centuries later, Jesus said, " 'Any city or house divided against itself shall not stand' " (Matt. 12:25b). If believers today want to be effective servants of Christ, they must do as the Israelites did—put away insignificant differences, unite on essentials, and march arm in arm against their common foes.

D. They abandoned themselves to the plan as they fixed their attention on the Lord. The Israelites' response to Joshua's orders was clear and affirming:

> "All that you have commanded us we will do, and wherever you send us we will go. Just as we obeyed Moses in all things, so we will obey you; only may the Lord your God be with you, as He was with Moses. Anyone who rebels against your command and does not obey your words in all that you command him, shall be put to death; only be strong and courageous." (Josh. 1:16b–18)

It seems incredible that the offspring of independent, stubborn, and rebellious nomads would commit themselves so completely to Joshua. What made the difference between this generation and the one that died in the wilderness? The answer is found in their spiritual perspective. Unlike their forefathers, the new generation of Israelites had their eyes firmly focused on the Lord. They had seen that He was serious about His requirement for obedience from His people. Also, for forty years in the wilderness they had witnessed His faithfulness to them. With these experiences embedded in their memories, they unreservedly committed themselves to God and His chosen leader. This kind of dedication enabled them to make the adjustments necessary for uniting in strength. Likewise, when the Lord becomes the center of our undivided attention and devotion, we will see operation assimilation move from being a distant dream to an obtainable reality.

III. Assimilation Applied

The challenge before us is clear: We need to get serious about assimilation, particularly in our churches, with our acquaintances, and in one-on-one relationships. The three statements given below each reveal an appropriate application that can help us make assimilation a part of our lives.

A. In our churches, we need to pull together and ignore our petty differences.

B. With our acquaintances, we must be willing to reach out and risk relating.

C. In our one-on-one relationships, we must be willing to adapt and adjust as we become closer.

Living Insights

Study One

A serious student of the Bible learns the art of asking questions of the Scriptures. It's an essential ingredient in moving from observing what the text says to interpreting what it means. Let's try our hand at this Bible study method.

• Turn to Joshua 1. After reading its eighteen verses, copy the following chart into your notebook. The left-hand column contains the six basic questions that will start you off as you use the center column to write specific questions related to the passage. Then proceed to the right-hand column and jot down the answers. Try to find your answers in Joshua 1. If you need additional help, consult other biblical passages or a Bible dictionary.[2]

General Questions	Specific Questions	Specific Answers
Who?		
What?		
Where?		
When?		
Why?		
How?		

2. Some helpful Bible dictionaries are: *Unger's Bible Dictionary,* by Merrill F. Unger, rev. ed. (Chicago: Moody Press, 1966); *The Zondervan Pictorial Bible Dictionary* (Grand Rapids, Mich.: Regency Reference Library, Zondervan Publishing House, 1967); and *Nelson's Illustrated Bible Dictionary* (Nashville: Thomas Nelson Publishers, 1986).

🐾 Living Insights

How familiar are you with the concept of assimilation? Whether you've just been introduced to it or have known about it for years, let's give assimilation some time for consideration.

● Take the next few minutes to think about the following questions. The answers may seem simple at first, but look more deeply and search out some additional thoughts.

—How would I define *assimilation?*

—How can I demonstrate assimilation in my life over the next week? The next month?

⚒ Digging Deeper

Our discussion of assimilation raises at least two questions that deserve to be explored: (1) What are the essentials on which Christians can unite? (2) What are the enemies Christians should be fighting against? Since the first century A.D., believers have had disagreements on a variety of issues. Christians have broken ranks over such matters as the appropriate mode of baptism, the correct form of church government, and the exact placement of Christ's Second Advent in the Bible's depiction of end-time events. Traditionally, however, believers have remained united on the central doctrines of the Christian faith:

—God is the Creator and Sustainer of the universe

—Jesus Christ is God the Son and the Redeemer of mankind

—the Bible is God's Word

—salvation comes by faith alone

—Jesus Christ was born of a virgin, died on a cross, rose physically from the dead, and ascended to heaven

—one day, Christ will return in power to rule

Christians have historically upheld these beliefs as the essentials of Christianity, believing that the very foundation of their faith rests on the validity of these doctrines. Since their earliest days, Christians have also united to battle a number of common enemies. Usually these foes have been philosophical, theological, social, political, or spiritual in nature. In our present pluralistic society, believers are facing a vast number of challenges to their faith that can most effectively be met by a united and active Christian community. If you would like to dig deeper into the essentials of Christianity or prepare yourself to enter the battles being waged against Christianity's contemporary enemies, you will find the following sources to be a tremendous help.

- **Sources on Christianity's Essentials**

Balchin, John. *What Christians Believe.* A Lion Manual. Belleville, Mich.: Lion Publishing Corp., 1984. This book is designed especially for teenagers.

Bavinck, Herman. *The Doctrine of God.* Translated by William Hendriksen. Grand Rapids, Mich.: Baker Book House, 1977.

Carey, George. *A Tale of Two Churches: Can Protestants and Catholics Get Together?* Foreword by J. I. Packer. Downers Grove, Ill.: InterVarsity Press, 1985.

Craig, William Lane. *The Son Rises: The Historical Evidence for the Resurrection of Jesus.* Chicago: Moody Press, 1981.

Dobson, Edward. *In Search of Unity: An Appeal to Fundamentalists and Evangelicals.* Nashville: Thomas Nelson Publishers, 1985.

Eerdmans' Handbook to Christian Belief. Edited by Robin Keeley. Grand Rapids, Mich.: William B. Eerdmans Publishing Co., 1982.

Lewis, C. S. *Mere Christianity.* New York: Macmillan Publishing Co., 1952.

Lightner, Robert P. *The Death Christ Died: A Case for Unlimited Atonement.* Schaumburg, Ill.: Regular Baptist Press, 1967.

Little, Paul E. *Know What You Believe.* Wheaton, Ill.: Victor Books, 1969.

Machen, J. Gresham. *The Virgin Birth of Christ.* Reprint. Grand Rapids, Mich.: Baker Book House, 1965.

Martin, Ralph. *The Return of the Lord.* Ann Arbor, Mich.: Servant Books, 1983.

Martin, Walter. *Essential Christianity.* Rev. ed. Santa Ana, Calif.: Vision House Publishers, 1975.

Pache, René. *The Inspiration and Authority of Scripture.* Translated by Helen I. Needham. Chicago: Moody Press, 1969.

Packer, J. I. *The Apostles' Creed.* Wheaton, Ill.: Tyndale House Publishers, 1977.

———. *Knowing God.* Downers Grove, Ill.: InterVarsity Press, 1973.

Pentecost, J. Dwight. *Things Which Become Sound Doctrine.* Grand Rapids, Mich.: Zondervan Publishing House, 1970.

Stott, John R. W. *Basic Christianity.* Downers Grove, Ill.: InterVarsity Press, 1958.

Walvoord, John F. *Jesus Christ Our Lord.* Chicago: Moody Press, 1969.

Webber, Robert E. *Common Roots: A Call to Evangelical Maturity.* Grand Rapids, Mich.: Zondervan Publishing House, 1978.

- **Responses to Christianity's Enemies**

Bubeck, Mark I. *Overcoming the Adversary.* Chicago: Moody Press, 1984.

Cizik, Richard, ed. *The High Cost of Indifference: Can Christians Afford Not to Act?* Ventura, Calif.: Regal Books, 1984.

Colson, Charles. *Who Speaks for God? Confronting the World with Real Christianity.* Westchester, Ill.: Crossway Books, 1985.

Craig, William Lane. *Apologetics: An Introduction.* Chicago: Moody Press, 1984.

———. *The Existence of God and the Beginning of the Universe.* San Bernardino, Calif.: Here's Life Publishers, 1979.

Fowler, Richard A., and House, H. Wayne. *The Christian Confronts His Culture.* Chicago: Moody Press, 1983.

Geisler, Norman L., ed. *Biblical Errancy: An Analysis of Its Philosophical Roots.* Grand Rapids, Mich.: Zondervan Publishing House, 1981.

———. *Christian Apologetics.* Grand Rapids, Mich.: Baker Book House, 1976.

———. *False Gods of Our Time.* Eugene, Oreg.: Harvest House Publishers, 1985.

———. *Is Man the Measure? An Evaluation of Contemporary Humanism.* Grand Rapids, Mich.: Baker Book House, 1983.

———. and Watkins, William D. *Perspectives: Understanding and Evaluating Today's World Views.* San Bernardino, Calif.: Here's Life Publishers, 1984.

Groothuis, Douglas R. *Unmasking the New Age.* Downers Grove, Ill.: InterVarsity Press, 1986.

Gruenler, Royce Gordon. *The Inexhaustible God: Biblical Faith and the Challenge of Process Theism.* Grand Rapids, Mich.: Baker Book House, 1983.

Gundry, Stanley N., and Johnson, Alan F., eds. *Tensions in Contemporary Theology.* Rev. ed. Foreword by Roger Nicole. Chicago: Moody Press, 1979.

Kirk, J. Andrew. *Liberation Theology: An Evangelical View from the Third World.* New Foundations Theological Library. Atlanta: John Knox Press, 1979.

Lewis, Gordon, and Demarest, Bruce, eds. *Challenges to Inerrancy: A Theological Response.* Chicago: Moody Press, 1984.

Lutzer, Erwin W. *Exploding the Myths That Could Destroy America.* Foreword by John Warwick Montgomery. Chicago: Moody Press, 1986.

Martin, Walter. *The Kingdom of the Cults.* Rev. ed. Minneapolis: Bethany House Publishers, 1985.

———. *The New Cults.* Santa Ana, Calif.: Vision House, 1980.

McDowell, Josh, and Stewart, Don. *Handbook of Today's Religions.* San Bernardino, Calif.: Here's Life Publishers, 1983.

Núñez, Emilio A. *Liberation Theology.* Translated by Paul E. Sywulka. Chicago: Moody Press, 1985.

Passantino, Robert and Gretchen. *Answers to the Cultist at Your Door.* Foreword by Walter Martin. Eugene, Oreg.: Harvest House Publishers, 1981.

Schlossberg, Herbert. *Idols for Destruction: Christian Faith and Its Confrontation with American Society.* Nashville: Thomas Nelson Publishers, 1983.

Sproul, R. C. *Lifeviews: Understanding the Ideas That Shape Society Today.* A Crucial Questions Book. Old Tappan, N.J.: Fleming H. Revell Co., 1986.

Stedman, Ray C. *Spiritual Warfare: Winning the Daily Battle with Satan.* Portland: Multnomah Press, 1975.

Stott, John. *Involvement: Being a Responsible Christian in a Non-Christian Society.* Vol. 1. A Crucial Questions Book. Old Tappan, N.J.: Fleming H. Revell Co., 1985.

———. *Involvement: Social and Sexual Relationships in the Modern World.* Vol. 2. A Crucial Questions Book. Old Tappan, N.J.: Fleming H. Revell Co., 1985.

Unger, Merrill F. *Demons in the World Today.* Wheaton, Ill.: Tyndale House Publishers, 1971.

Varghese, Roy Abraham, ed. *The Intellectuals Speak Out about God: A Handbook for the Christian Student in a Secular Society.* Foreword by Ronald Reagan. Chicago: Regnery Gateway, 1984.

United and Invincible
Joshua 1, 6, 8, 10

Several centuries after the Exodus and the Hebrews' invasion of Canaan, King David ruled over the united nation of Israel. During his reign, he penned these words of timeless truth:

> How good and pleasant it is when brothers live together in unity!
> It is like precious oil poured on the head,
> > running down on the beard,
> > . . . down upon the collar of his robes.[1] (Ps. 133:1–2)

Theologically speaking, the bond believers have in Christ can bring about this kind of joy and peace. In spite of their differences in style, language, culture, color, and education, Christians can live together in harmony. And when they do, they become virtually invincible. A perfect example of unity and what it can bring is provided in Joshua's account of the conquest of Canaan. Let's turn our attention to this portion of Scripture and keep ourselves open to the truths it conveys.

I. The Biblical Basis of Unity

Before we flip the pages of our Bibles to Joshua's book, let's consider some key texts in the New Testament that lay the foundation for Christian unity. In 1 Corinthians the Apostle Paul clearly says that all who have been spiritually baptized into God's forever family are individual members of the Body of Christ (12:12–14, 27). The Head of this group is the resurrected Lord, Jesus Christ (Col. 1:18). He is the One who, through His death, made it possible for diverse peoples to come together as spiritual brothers and sisters (Eph. 2:11–22). But even He realized that spiritual and relational oneness do not always coexist. That is, although people may be bound together by one Savior, they do not automatically serve one another in familial love and respect. Perhaps this is why Jesus prayed that throughout time His followers would display the kind of harmony which exists between Him and His Heavenly Father (John 17:20–23). For when the Church manifests oneness to this extent, she provides confirmation to the world that Jesus was the Father's love-gift to mankind (v. 23). So, once we become members of God's family, we need to strive in humility to treat one another as spiritual kin. By relating to each other on this level, we will strengthen one another's Christian walk and effectiveness as beacons of light in a cold, dark world.

II. An Old Testament Portrait of Unity

Moving from the New Testament to the Old, we find a prime example of unity in Joshua. This book records the Israelites' conquest of Canaan. As we will soon discover, an essential element of the

---

1. *The NIV Study Bible* (Grand Rapids, Mich.: Zondervan Bible Publishers, 1985).

Hebrews' success was the willingness they showed to tackle their God-given task together. Their spirit of unity was manifested in at least four ways.

A. Without fear they rallied around their leader and the Lord. Standing on the threshold of a military campaign, the Hebrews expressed their support of Joshua and God's invasion plan. By looking closely at the content of their response, we can see several manifestations of their unity:

> "All that you have commanded us we will do [cooperation], and wherever you send us we will go [availability]. Just as we obeyed Moses in all things, so we will obey you [commitment]; only may the Lord your God be with you, as He was with Moses [hope]. Anyone who rebels against your command and does not obey your words in all that you command him, shall be put to death [loyalty]; only be strong and courageous [encouragement]." (Josh. 1:16–18)

A people characterized by oneness is not comprised of self-appointed critics or selfish complainers. Instead, such a group's conduct is marked by affirmation, allegiance, and a sense of corporate responsibility. The Israelites displayed these qualities in their words and deeds.

B. Without resistance they accepted an unusual strategy. After moving into the Promised Land, the Hebrews faced their first formidable challenge—the conquest of Jericho. With its massive outer wall and valiant army, the city was practically impregnable. But this obstacle did not lessen the Hebrews' willingness to carry out Joshua's directives. Without any hint of doubt or resistance, the people obeyed Joshua's command to march around Jericho once each day for six days straight, to march around it seven times on the seventh day, and to shout loudly when they heard the trumpets sound off (6:2–20). Once they had followed these instructions, they saw the wall of Jericho collapse, making it possible for them to take the city (vv. 20b–25). By standing united in obedience to God and His chosen leader, they became an invincible force through which the Lord could carry out His work.

C. Without jealousy they worked as a team to accomplish objectives. The next victory the Hebrews experienced was at the city of Ai. This time, however, the military strategy involved an ambush. Joshua commanded some of the people to prepare to attack Ai from its back side (8:4). He told another group to join him in a march against the front side of the city—a move that would result in a temporary retreat. This act was designed to get the enemy forces away from Ai so that the rest of the

Israelites could attack the city from the rear unchallenged (vv. 5–8). When the Hebrews heard the plan, nobody asked, "Now who will get the credit for the victory?" They obeyed their orders as a team of individuals committed to one another. Humility and cooperation, not pride and competition, pervaded their ranks. As a result, Ai fell according to the plan (vv. 10–28).

D. Without doubting they trusted God to assist them. Soon after the defeat of Ai, some allies of the Hebrews were attacked by the Amorites (10:1–5). When Joshua received word of the assault, he assembled the Israelites and led them on an all-night march to the battlefront (vv. 6–9). The Lord had promised him that not even one Amorite would prevail against him (v. 8). Resting on God's word, Joshua led the Hebrews into the fray. What happened was nothing short of miraculous:

> And the Lord confounded the Amorites before Israel, and He slew them with a great slaughter at Gibeon, and pursued them by the way of the ascent of Bethhoron, and struck them as far as Azekah and Makkedah. And it came about as they fled from before Israel, while they were at the descent of Bethhoron, that the Lord threw large stones from heaven on them as far as Azekah, and they died; there were more who died from the hailstones than those whom the sons of Israel killed with the sword. Then Joshua spoke to the Lord in the day when the Lord delivered up the Amorites before the sons of Israel, and he said in the sight of Israel,
>
> "O sun, stand still at Gibeon,
> And O moon in the valley of Aijalon."
> So the sun stood still, and the moon stopped,
> Until the nation avenged themselves of
> their enemies.
>
> Is it not written in the book of Jashar? And the sun stopped in the middle of the sky, and did not hasten to go down for about a whole day. And there was no day like that before it or after it, when the Lord listened to the voice of a man; for the Lord fought for Israel. Then Joshua and all Israel with him returned to the camp to Gilgal.[2] (vv. 10–15)

2. A good deal of speculation surrounds the miracle of the prolonged day that is recorded in this passage. Two helpful discussions of this miracle and the explanations that have been offered for it can be found in *The Christian View of Science and Scripture*, by Bernard Ramm (Grand Rapids, Mich.: William B. Eerdmans Publishing Co., 1954), pp. 107–10, and in the *Encyclopedia of Bible Difficulties*, by Gleason L. Archer, foreword by Kenneth S. Kantzer (Grand Rapids, Mich.: Zondervan Publishing House, 1982), pp. 161–62.

Joshua and his troops were convinced that God would do what He said He would. As they acted on His promise, they became an unconquerable force.

III. Some Crucial Thoughts to Consider

We have seen that God desires His people to become united and that He accomplishes great things through them when they do work together. These facts should encourage us to make harmony in the Body of Christ a corporate and personal goal. With this in mind, let's consider two thoughts that can help us turn the idea of unity into a day-to-day reality.

A. Regarding our churches, the pursuit of unity is hard' work, but it's well worth the effort. Christian leaders and followers need to strive to develop and maintain a sense of oneness in their local assemblies (Eph. 4:1–3). It's true that this task is sometimes difficult and frustrating, but keeping in mind what its accomplishment brings will give the impetus we need to press on (vv. 11–16).

B. Regarding our personal lives, humility is of the highest value, but it's rarely seen. We cannot achieve unity in our churches until we begin to put away our pride and to serve others unselfishly. Lust, greed, and envy are the enemies of Christian harmony (James 4:1–2). We can overcome them by getting our eyes off ourselves and by seeing others through the eyes of Christ.

Living Insights

Study One

The story of Joshua leading the conquest of Canaan is inspiring. It's exciting to see how God caused the Hebrews to be unified and invincible.

- Let's read this story again. This time, however, let's read it in a different version of Scripture—another translation, or perhaps even a paraphrase. Whichever version you choose, take an unhurried look at the following passages in Joshua: 1:16–18, 6:1–21, 8:1–29, and 10:1–14.

🐾 *Living Insights*

Unity and invincibility are worth thinking about further. Gather together your family or a group of friends in order to discuss these two important concepts. Use the questions and ideas below to stimulate your thinking.

—Define *unity* in your own words. Then expound on your definition by adding a few more thoughts.

—Why are we by nature rigid rather than free? Why are we more narrow than open in our acceptance of others? Discuss your answers.

—Name some ways you could begin to develop unity among your family, friends, and fellow Christians.

—Discuss the need for affirmation. Can you recall a time when someone affirmed you and renewed your spirit? Share it.

—Talk about jealousy. Is this one of your battles? Have you ever borne the brunt of someone else's jealous assault? How can jealousy be conquered? Discuss some specific steps you can take to overcome jealousy in your own life.

When the Fellowship Breaks Down
Joshua 7

Growing closer together sounds great . . . and it is. But we must not deceive ourselves into thinking that building relationships always goes smoothly. There will come times when friction and disharmony will occur in even the best of Christian fellowships. This truth has been verified throughout history, but just a cursory glance at the first-century Church yields all the supporting evidence needed. For example, in the early days of the Jerusalem church, "a complaint arose on the part of the Hellenistic Jews against the native Hebrews, because their widows were being overlooked in the daily serving of food" (Acts 6:1b). On another occasion, the twelve apostles temporarily refused to offer the hand of fellowship to a new convert because of his former anti-Christian activities (9:26). Somewhat later, the first major Church council was convened in order to settle some doctrinal disputes between believers (15:1–35). In short, we can count on the fact that conflicts will arise. The questions we need to address are: Why *do* conflicts arise? and How should we respond to them? Studying the biblical answers will help us understand and work through breakdowns in relationships in a way that will strengthen the unity of the Body of Christ.

I. Some Reasons Fellowship Breaks Down

There are several situations that bring about isolation or division in relationships. Let's consider five of the more common reasons individuals pull away from one another.

A. Extreme suffering or sickness.
Most of us seek to be alone when we are hurting. Our pain may be physical, emotional, psychological, or even spiritual, but if it is great enough, we will usually retreat from life's relational demands (see Job 2:11–13, Matt. 26:36–44).

B. Burnout and fatigue.
People who burn the candle at both ends frequently end up dropping out of their frenzied way of life. And so they should, for part of the cure for this kind of exhaustion is rest and relaxation. In time, most burnout victims will replenish their energy and gain a renewed perspective on life. But without a decrease in responsibilities, including relational ones, these individuals are headed for serious consequences, among which is frequently an untimely death (see 1 Kings 19:1–8).

C. Trouble at home or personal turmoil.
Domestic friction, financial upheavals, moral compromises—difficulties such as these often cause us to isolate and insulate ourselves. And yet by running from our hurt and worry, we are putting ourselves in the position of facing the guilt, bitterness, anxiety, and pain all alone— a position that only intensifies our struggle (see Ps. 32:3–5).

D. Friction between two or more individuals. Conflicts that arise between friends, associates in ministry, fellow employees, and the like are frequently the most difficult to resolve. This is especially so if one of the individuals involved was burned when he or she sincerely reached out to the other party. A person who has been offended in this way is "harder to be won than a strong city" (Prov. 18:19a).

E. Open disobedience toward God. Probably no cause of isolation and division brings greater harm and shame to the Church than does blatant defiance toward God. Disobedience hurts everyone, not just the rebel. For it raises questions about the integrity and morality of *all* Christians.

II. Ai and the Hebrews

A biblical illustration of one person's rebellion against God affecting the whole body is found in Joshua 7. Following the defeat of Jericho, the Hebrews set their sights on conquering Ai—a city that posed a far less difficult military challenge than Jericho did. The Israelites were so confident they could take Ai that they convinced their leader, Joshua, to send only a few thousand men to fight against it (Josh. 7:2–3). The biblical text records what happened:

> So about three thousand men from the people went up there, but they fled from the men of Ai. And the men of Ai struck down about thirty-six of their men, and pursued them from the gate as far as Shebarim, and struck them down on the descent, so the hearts of the people melted and became as water. (vv. 4–5)

What went wrong? Why did the Israelites lose this battle? The remainder of the account reveals the answer and exposes the four stages we must work through to restore any broken relationship.

A. The symptom stage: "Something is wrong." Two things about the Hebrews' attack on Ai indicate that there was division in their midst. First, there was a break in their normal routine. Before battling Ai, they had arisen victorious in warfare. In their confrontation with Ai, they fell back in defeat, even though their foe was significantly less formidable than the enemy they had previously encountered. Second, the Israelites became discouraged and distraught over their military setback. Similar symptoms occur when our relationships begin to suffer. The person who always came around and shared freely begins to shy away and speak guardedly. The change in routine indicates that something is wrong. Moreover, as the distance between individuals grows, so does discouragement and frustration. If left to itself, the once vibrant and valuable relationship will become lifeless and worthless.

37

B. The concern stage: "What has happened?" In response to the Hebrews' defeat, Joshua tore his clothes in humiliation and bowed before the Lord with the elders of Israel, offering a prayer marked by bewilderment and fear (vv. 6–9). Likewise, when we are in desperate and confusing situations, we frequently turn to close friends and seek God in prayer. By doing so, we often find strength, solace, and insight that would otherwise be absent. This was certainly true for Joshua and his prayer partners. As the text states, God answered their petitions by both unveiling the mystery surrounding their military loss and telling them what they were supposed to do in response to the information He gave them:

> So the Lord said to Joshua, "Rise up! Why is it that you have fallen on your face? Israel has sinned, and they have also transgressed My covenant which I commanded them. And they have even taken some of the things under the ban and have both stolen and deceived. Moreover, they have also put them among their own things. Therefore the sons of Israel cannot stand before their enemies; they turn their backs before their enemies, for they have become accursed. I will not be with you anymore unless you destroy the things under the ban from your midst. Rise up! Consecrate the people and say, 'Consecrate yourselves for tomorrow, for thus the Lord, the God of Israel, has said, "There are things under the ban in your midst, O Israel. You cannot stand before your enemies until you have removed the things under the ban from your midst." In the morning then you shall come near by your tribes. And it shall be that the tribe which the Lord takes by lot shall come near by families, and the family which the Lord takes shall come near by households, and the household which the Lord takes shall come near man by man. And it shall be that the one who is taken with the things under the ban shall be burned with fire, he and all that belongs to him, because he has transgressed the covenant of the Lord, and because he has committed a disgraceful thing in Israel.' " (vv. 10–15)

One individual's disobedience to a divine directive (cf. 6:18–19) had adversely affected all the Hebrew people. He had to be found and punished. The Lord told Joshua how this person could be identified and in what manner he was to be disciplined. It was up to Joshua to carry out God's instructions.

C. The discovery stage: "Who is involved?" The Israelite leader followed God's directions to the letter. His probe led him to the man who was responsible for all the havoc—Achan (7:16–18).

> So Achan answered Joshua and said, "Truly, I have sinned against the Lord, the God of Israel, and this is what I did: when I saw among the spoil a beautiful mantle from Shinar and two hundred shekels of silver and a bar of gold fifty shekels in weight, then I coveted them and took them; and behold, they are concealed in the earth inside my tent with the silver underneath it." (vv. 20–21)

Joshua confronted Achan in love, and Achan confessed with honesty. The encounter must have been a painful one, but it was obviously conducted in the right spirit. How important it is for us to learn how to compassionately admonish someone! For there will probably come a time when we will be obligated to rebuke a fellow believer who has sinned. And when such an occasion arises, we must be sure that we confront this individual in a biblical and loving way. Indeed, the *way* we carry out this task is as important as our obedience in doing it (cf. Matt. 18:15–17, 1 Cor. 6:1–7, Gal. 6:1–2, James 5:19–20).[1]

D. The assistance stage: "What is needed?" Once the rebel in the Israelite camp had been exposed, there was no question about what had to be done. In obedience to God's command, Achan and his children were killed and their bodies and possessions destroyed (Josh. 7:24–25).[2] With judgment meted out, "the Lord turned from the fierceness of His anger" (v. 26a). This account shows us that although the Lord is a God of grace and forgiveness, He is also a God of righteousness and justice. Therefore, He cannot condone sin. He must eradicate it, and He will not rest until every trace of rebellion has been removed from His people and His creation (cf. Rom. 8, Eph. 5:25–27, Jude 24,

---

1. Some helpful sources on confronting others in love are these: *Creative Conflict: How to Confront and Stay Friends,* by Joyce Huggett (Downers Grove, Ill.: InterVarsity Press, 1984); *When Caring Is Not Enough: Resolving Conflicts through Fair Fighting,* by David Augsburger (Ventura, Calif.: Regal Books, 1983); *Healing the Wounded: The Costly Love of Church Discipline,* by John White and Ken Blue, foreword by Ray C. Stedman (Downers Grove, Ill.: InterVarsity Press, 1985); *A Guide to Church Discipline,* by J. Carl Laney (Minneapolis, Minn.: Bethany House Publishers, 1985); *Restoring Fellowship,* by Joy P. Gage and Kenneth G. Gage (Chicago: Moody Press, 1984).

2. Bible expositor Donald K. Campbell (in "Joshua," from *The Bible Knowledge Commentary: Old Testament Edition,* eds. John F. Walvoord and Roy B. Zuck [Wheaton, Ill.: Victor Books, 1985], p. 345) writes this concerning the execution of Achan's children: "Since children were not to be executed for their father's sins (Deut. 24:16) it is assumed that Achan's family (except for his wife, who was not mentioned) were accomplices in the crime" (cf. Num. 16:28–35).

and the Revelation to John). As C. S. Lewis points out, this divine activity naturally flows from the Essence of love, who is God Himself:

> Love, in its own nature, demands the perfecting of the beloved; that the mere "kindness" which tolerates anything except suffering in its object is, in that respect, at the opposite pole from Love. When we fall in love with a woman, do we cease to care whether she is clean or dirty, fair or foul? Do we not rather then first begin to care? Does any woman regard it as a sign of love in a man that he neither knows nor cares how she is looking? Love may, indeed, love the beloved when her beauty is lost: but not because it is lost. Love may forgive all infirmities and love still in spite of them: but Love cannot cease to will their removal. Love is more sensitive than hatred itself to every blemish in the beloved.... Of all powers he forgives most, but he condones least: he is pleased with little, but demands all.
>
> When Christianity says that God loves man, it means that God *loves* man: not that He has some "disinterested" concern for our welfare, but that, in awful and surprising truth, we are the objects of His love.[3]

Because God is love and expects us to love others as He loves us (1 John 4:7–11), we will, on occasion, have to confront someone who has sinned. Although this is never a pleasant task, it is necessary, and one that is always to be carried out with the best interests of the offender in mind (1 Cor. 13:4–8a).

III. Ai and Us

Reflecting on what we have learned in this lesson, we can make at least three applications.

A. Most breakdowns in relationships that are the result of open disobedience toward God will not heal themselves—therefore, we need to get involved in the restoration process.

B. The longer the breakdown persists, the greater the negative impact becomes—therefore, we need to begin to restore the fellowship as soon as possible.

C. Solutions will be initially painful, but ultimately rewarding—therefore, we should never give up striving for resolutions and renewals.

---

3. C. S. Lewis, *The Problem of Pain* (New York: Macmillan Publishing Co., 1962), p. 46.

Living Insights

Study One

Confrontation is seldom pleasant, but the Scriptures have much to say about its necessity. In our study, we concentrated on the seventh chapter of Joshua. Now let's cross over to the New Testament and survey some of what it says on this subject.

- Copy the following chart into your notebook. Then, as you look up each reference, jot down observations that are pertinent to our study of confrontation.

What to Do When Fellowship Breaks Down	
References	Observations on Confrontation
1 Corinthians 6:1–5	
Galatians 6:1–2	
Ephesians 4:15, 25–32	
James 5:19–20	

Living Insights

Study Two

Because the family of God is like a human body, it can break down from fatigue, neglect, or abuse. So, let's practice some preventive medicine in order to keep the Body healthy.

- Listed on the next page are some of the more common reasons for the breakdown of fellowship. How can you help prevent these breakdowns from happening in your life and the lives of others? Do you know someone who might be drifting away from you or other believers because of one of these problems? How can you reach out and be God's instrument of healing? Take some time to record your answers in your notebook. Then take the steps necessary to begin putting shoe leather on your responses. After all, medicine is a worthless cure if it is never given to those who need it.

Continued on next page

My Role in Keeping the Body Healthy

Causes of Breakdowns	Ways I Can Help
Extreme suffering and sickness	
Burnout and fatigue	
Trouble at home or personal turmoil	
Friction between two or more individuals	
Open disobedience toward God	

Authentic Love

1 Corinthians 13:1–8a

A number of years ago, Hal David and Burt Bacharach composed a song that captured the world's feeling of loneliness and hunger for love. In part, the lyrics said:

> Lord, we don't need another mountain.
> There are mountains and hillsides enough to climb.
> There are oceans and rivers enough to cross . . . enough to last
>   'til the end of time.
> What the world needs now is love, sweet love;
> No, not just for some but for everyone. . . .
> It's the only thing that there's just too little of.[1]

Their message still rings true today—we *do* need love. But what kind of love do we need? Christian scholar C. S. Lewis distinguishes between four types of love. *Eros*-love is "that state which we call 'being in love'; or, if you prefer, that kind of love which lovers are 'in.' "[2] *Affection*-love gives thanks for and takes delight in the objects of its admiration. *Friendship*-love is that deep-felt sense of togetherness and joy two people have with one another. Finally, *gift*-love is the expression of devotion that longs to give what is best and to serve regardless of the cost.[3] It is the fourth kind of love—what the Bible calls *àgápe* love—that we need most of all. It finds its fullest expression in God's relationship to us. Take redemption, for example. When we were unlovable, God sent His only Son to die on the cross so that we could receive His fulness forever (John 3:16–17, Rom. 5:6–11, 1 John 4:9–10). Although God did not need to love us (Acts 17:25), He chose to meet our desperate need for love by making the highest sacrifice He could—the giving of His own Son's life. With this great truth of salvation in mind, the Apostle John writes, "Beloved, if God so loved us, we also ought to love one another" (1 John 4:11). Indeed, the heartbeat of healthy, open relationships is àgápe love. Therefore, it is àgápe love—the highest expression of authentic love—that we will concentrate on.

I. Some Expressions of Inauthentic Love

Before looking at some of the positive aspects of àgápe love, let's become aware of some of its counterfeit expressions. This will help us avoid those traps that threaten to divert our pursuit and practice of authentic love.

A. The gusher. The gusher is a person who dumps nice-sounding superlatives on others with a sweet, syrupy smile. His compliments

---

1. "What the World Needs Now Is Love." Words by Hal David and music by Burt Bacharach (New York: Blue Seas Music, Inc.; Jac Music Co., 1965).

2. C. S. Lewis, *The Four Loves* (New York: Harcourt Brace Jovanovich, 1960), p. 131.

3. Lewis, *The Four Loves,* chaps. 3, 4, 6.

often inflate egos, making people feel good for the moment, but behind his flattery there is no depth of feeling or commitment—only worthless froth. Authentic lovers, however, speak with integrity. They seek to edify, but not at the expense of sacrificing the truth. Their love is honest and dependable.

B. The pressurizer. An individual who has a you-scratch-my-back-and-I'll-scratch-yours kind of love falls into the category of "the pressurizer." He uses love to manipulate others into giving him what he wants. 'Agápe love, on the other hand, has no hidden agendas or selfish motives. Its goal is to set people free to be all they can be, not to use them to fulfill selfish dreams.

C. The ramrod. The ramrod lover pushes himself onto others. Rather than taking into account the needs and desires of other people, he runs roughshod over them, determined only to express and satisfy his own passion. In contrast, true love never forces its way into the lives of others. It seeks to sensitively persuade, woo, and uplift the objects of its concern and care.

II. An Analysis of Authentic Love

Leaving the false expressions of love behind, let's turn to àgápe love—gift-love—and reflect on it in relationship to our own lives. The biblical passage that best expresses the necessity and essence of àgápe love is 1 Corinthians 13:1–8a. Take a few moments to ponder these words from the Apostle Paul:

> If I speak with the tongues of men and of angels, but do not have love, I have become a noisy gong or a clanging cymbal. And if I have the gift of prophecy, and know all mysteries and all knowledge; and if I have all faith, so as to remove mountains, but do not have love, I am nothing. And if I give all my possessions to feed the poor, and if I deliver my body to be burned, but do not have love, it profits me nothing. Love is patient, love is kind, and is not jealous; love does not brag and is not arrogant, does not act unbecomingly; it does not seek its own, is not provoked, does not take into account a wrong suffered, does not rejoice in unrighteousness, but rejoices with the truth; bears all things, believes all things, hopes all things, endures all things. Love never fails.

In this passage we find four truths about love that help us see its value in developing unguarded relationships.

A. Love is essential, not optional. The first three verses convey this truth. Three times Paul states, "but do not have love." And following each of these instances, he adds a poignant conclusion: "I have become a noisy gong or a clanging cymbal ... I am nothing ... It profits me nothing." In other words, a relationship without love is like a car without wheels, a train without a locomotive, or a house without a foundation. Take away love, and our lives and relationships equal zero. The force of Paul's thought is brought out in the following paraphrase:

> If I have the ability to speak in polished and impressive fashion, or
>
> If I can utter sounds only angels understand, or
>
> If I have such a pronounced prophetic gift that I know the entire future . . . everything about everything, or
>
> If I possess such unswerving faith so that I can remove mountains,
>
> If I am so genuinely sacrificial that all my possessions are given away to the needy, or even
>
> If I commit the supreme act of unselfishness and go to the gas chamber for the sake of the gospel, and yet lack love, the essential ingredient; then,
>
> All my speaking has the sound of a hollow basin of brass and
>
> All my knowledge and faith is of no use and
>
> All my philanthropy and martyrdom gains *nothing* at all![4]

Some Probing Questions

Is àgápe love an essential ingredient in your life? Do you place a high premium on its development in your relationships? Would your family, your work associates, and others who are close to you agree that your life is characterized by authentic love?

B. Love is a demonstration, not an inclination. True love is not just *desiring* what is best for others, but also *doing* what is best for them. Action, involvement, responsiveness—these are the hallmarks of genuine love. Paul communicates this by describing love in active terms: "patient . . . kind . . . rejoices with the truth; bears all things, believes all things, hopes all things, endures all things" (vv. 4–7). This description shows us that the opposite of love is not hate—for hate is at least active—but indifference or apathy.

---

4. Charles R. Swindoll, *Dropping Your Guard: The Value of Open Relationships* (Waco, Tex.: Word Books, 1983), p. 120.

C. Love is a magnet that draws us together, not a wall that keeps us apart. There is nothing in Paul's description of love that is offensive. In fact, àgápe love is so centered on the welfare of others that even extremely selfish individuals will at least occasionally give in to its promptings and enjoy its benefits. We can readily see why this occurs by considering five statements that summarize the fifteen characteristics of love Paul gives. We might call these the ABCs of authentic love:

I *accept* people as they are.
I *believe* people are valuable.
I *care* when others hurt.
I *desire* only what is best for others.
I *erase* all offenses.

D. Love is a long-term investment, not a quick-return loan. There is nothing shallow or short about àgápe love. It "bears all things, believes all things, hopes all things, endures all things . . . [and] never fails" (vv. 7–8a). It is tough love, unconditional love, long-suffering love, resilient love. When the sea of life becomes rough and dangerous, authentic love does not retreat, but seeks to navigate through the storm, trusting in God to see it through.

III. A Decision We Each Must Make

It should be clear from what we have discovered that ágápe love cannot be obtained apart from a growing personal relationship with Jesus Christ. Only through Him do we receive the Holy Spirit and the fruit of His power: "[ágápe] love, joy, peace, patience, kindness, goodness, faithfulness, gentleness, [and] self-control" (Gal. 5:22–23a). Therefore, if we want to personally experience and publicly express authentic love, we must give ourselves to Christ in faith. And once we are His, we must submit ourselves to the Spirit's control (vv. 16–26, Eph. 5:18). Of course, we can refuse to embark on "the road less traveled"—the road of genuine Christian love. After all, the ágápe way demands personal sacrifice and opens us up to potential heartache and abuse. How much easier it would be to keep to ourselves, striving to satisfy only our own needs and wants. And yet, as C. S. Lewis points out, the toll of living a self-centered life can be extremely high:

> There is no safe investment. To love at all is to be vulnerable. Love anything, and your heart will certainly be wrung and possibly be broken. If you want to make sure of keeping it intact, you must give your heart to no one, not even to an animal. Wrap it carefully round with hobbies and little luxuries; avoid all entanglements; lock it up safe in the casket or coffin of your selfishness. But in that casket—safe, dark, motionless, airless—it will change. It will not be broken; it will become unbreakable, impenetrable, irredeemable. The alternative to tragedy, or at least to the risk of tragedy, is damnation. The only place outside Heaven where you can be perfectly safe from all the dangers and perturbations of love is Hell.[5]

Which road will you choose to travel? The road of selfishness or the road of selflessness? Only the latter path leads to the best God has to offer.

Continued on next page

---

5. Lewis, *The Four Loves*, p. 169.

🎋 *Living Insights*

Our study includes a very meaningful paraphrase of the first few verses of 1 Corinthians 13—one of the most familiar chapters in all of Scripture. Let's use our own creativity to dig into verses 4–8a.

● Copy the following chart into your notebook. Then write a definition of each trait listed below. You may want to look up other passages or consult a Bible dictionary for additional help.

1 Corinthians 13:4–8a	
'Agápe Love . . .	My Descriptions
Is patient	
Is kind	
Is not jealous	
Does not brag	
Is not arrogant	
Does not act unbecomingly	
Does not seek its own	
Is not provoked	
Does not take into account a wrong suffered	
Does not rejoice in unrighteousness	
Rejoices with the truth	
Bears all things	
Believes all things	
Hopes all things	
Endures all things	
Never fails	

🌳 *Living Insights*

Now that you've had some time to reflect on 1 Corinthians 13, proceed one step further in order to personalize this text.

- The following chart will help you move from description to application. For each trait listed, answer the question, "How can I begin to express this quality in my life during the next week?" Try to be specific in your answers.

1 Corinthians 13:4–8a	
'Agápe Love . . .	My Plans
Is patient	
Is kind	
Is not jealous	
Does not brag	
Is not arrogant	
Does not act unbecomingly	
Does not seek its own	
Is not provoked	
Does not take into account a wrong suffered	
Does not rejoice in unrighteousness	
Rejoices with the truth	
Bears all things	
Believes all things	
Hopes all things	
Endures all things	
Never fails	

Needed: Shelter for Storm Victims
Selected Scripture

You have just found out that your son is a practicing homosexual. Or your mate has told you that he or she loves someone else and wants to divorce you. Or perhaps your daughter has run away for the third time . . . you have just been fired from your job . . . your drug habit has pushed you to the brink of despair . . . you are near a nervous breakdown . . . or you have recently learned that, though unmarried, you are pregnant. What do you do when the bottom drops out of your life? Who can you turn to for understanding and comfort, affirmation and hope? Is there a shelter—a place of refuge—where you will be welcomed rather than judged? Yes, there is. But all too often it is the neighborhood bar, not the local church. Bruce Larson and Keith Miller lament this fact in revealing words:

> The neighborhood bar is possibly the best counterfeit there is to the fellowship Christ wants to give His church. It's an imitation, dispensing liquor instead of grace, escape rather than reality, but it is a permissive, accepting, and inclusive fellowship. It is unshockable. It is democratic. You can tell people secrets and they usually don't tell others or even want to. The bar flourishes not because most people are alcoholics, but because God has put into the human heart the desire to know and be known, to love and be loved, and so many seek a counterfeit at the price of a few beers.
>
> With all my heart I believe that Christ wants His church to be . . . a fellowship where people can come in and say, "I'm sunk!" "I'm beat!" "I've had it!"[1]

There will be times in each of our lives when we will be storm victims in need of shelter. There will also come times when other people will need us to offer them refuge. Because the fulfillment of these needs involves a willingness to be vulnerable and caring—in a word, unguarded—we will dig into the Scriptures to see what help they can give us in turning our lives and churches into dispensers of grace.

I. Shelter: When One Person Needed It

Throughout history, people—even believers—have needed places of refuge. A biblical illustration of one man who experienced this need is found in Psalm 31. While suffering greatly, the Israelite king David reached out to God for help:

> In Thee, O Lord, I have taken refuge;
> Let me never be ashamed;

---

1. Bruce Larson and Keith Miller, *The Edge of Adventure* (Waco, Tex.: Word Books, 1974), as quoted by Charles R. Swindoll in *Dropping Your Guard: The Value of Open Relationships* (Waco, Tex.: Word Books, 1983), p. 128.

In Thy righteousness deliver me.
Incline Thine ear to me, rescue me quickly;
Be Thou to me a rock of strength,
A stronghold to save me. (vv. 1–2)

The Hebrew term translated *refuge* refers to a place of safety or protection. When used figuratively, as it is in this passage, it means "putting confident trust in something or someone that can offer escape or protection from serious trouble."[2] David placed his trust in God; the Lord was his way of escape, his safety from danger. But what were the circumstances that prompted David to run to God? Let's consider them, for each one will also give us good reason to seek safety in the Lord.

A. He was in distress, and sorrow accompanied him. David expressed his condition in graphic terms: "Be gracious to me, O Lord, for I am in distress;/My eye is wasted away from grief, my soul and my body also./For my life is spent with sorrow,/And my years with sighing" (vv. 9–10a). Depressed, forlorn, and emotionally drained, David slumped into the compassionate arms of the Lord. How deeply God desires for us to turn to Him when we are "spent with sorrow"!

B. He had committed sin, and guilt accused him. "My strength has failed because of my iniquity," lamented David, "and my body has wasted away" (v. 10b). The embarrassment and shame that usually follows transgression often pains and debilitates us. In situations like this, we need grace and forgiveness. And who offers these mercies more faithfully than God?

C. He was surrounded by adversaries, and misunderstanding assaulted him. David grieved over the fact that his enemies had caused him to be ridiculed, criticized, rejected, slandered, and threatened (vv. 11–13). Even his own neighbors had spoken and acted against him. No wonder David sought someone who could offer him protection and relief. When we are condemned and abused by others, we too need to find someone who will seek to heal our wounds and guard us from further harm.

II. Refuge: How the Hebrews Provided It

Turning farther back in the Old Testament, we discover that not only did the Lord act as a refuge for His people, but He instructed them to also be a refuge for those in need. This comes out clearly in Joshua 20. There we learn that after the conquest of Canaan, the

---

2. See *Theological Wordbook of the Old Testament,* 2 vols., eds. R. Laird Harris, Gleason L. Archer, Jr., and Bruce K. Waltke (Chicago: Moody Press, 1980), vol. 1, pp. 307–8.

Israelites were to establish cities which were set apart as places of protection and relief. Let's examine this chapter more closely.

A. Commanded by God. The Lord instructed the Hebrews' leader, Joshua, to set aside certain cities as places of refuge for people who unintentionally killed someone. Manslayers needed a place where they could be protected from anyone who sought revenge (vv. 1–3). As Old Testament scholar Merrill F. Unger points out, the Hebrews took God's command seriously:

> According to the [rabbis], in order to aid the fugitive it was the business of the Sanhedrin to keep the roads leading to the cities of refuge in the best possible repair. No hills were left, every river was bridged, and the road itself was to be at least thirty-two cubits broad [about 48 feet wide]. At every turn were guide posts bearing the word *Refuge;* and two students of the law were appointed to accompany the fleeing man, to pacify, if possible, the avenger, should he overtake the fugitive.[3]

From Numbers 35 we learn that the Levites, the priestly class, were to receive forty-eight cities in which to live, and six of these were to be cities of refuge. In other words, both places and people were provided to aid the fugitive. The Lord wanted His people to make every effort to assist those who were in serious trouble.

B. Procedure for entrance. Individuals who fled to these six cities were required to present their cases before the elders who sat at the gates. These men were the civic leaders who, as part of their job, judged whether a person's offense qualified him to take advantage of their city's safety. And, of course, the only fugitives who were given asylum were those who had made tragic mistakes—people who had committed unintentional and unpremeditated offenses (vv. 16–24). Once the elders had given their approval, they permitted the fugitive to enter the city and gave him a place to live within its protective walls (Josh. 20:4).

C. Protection from avengers. After a fugitive had been admitted into a city of refuge, a trial was held to discover whether or not he was guilty of murder. If found innocent, he had to remain within the boundaries of the city to which he had fled in order to receive the city's protection. There he would have to live until the high priest died, at which time he could legally return to his former home (Num. 35:24–25, 28a; Josh. 20:6). However, if a manslayer was declared innocent of murder and

---

3. Merrill F. Unger, "Cities of Refuge," in *Unger's Bible Dictionary,* rev. ed. (Chicago: Moody Press, 1966), p. 208.

at some point left a city of refuge before the high priest's death, he could be legally slain by the blood avenger—a member of the victim's family who had been given the responsibility of avenging the victim's death (Num. 35:26–28a).[4] Moreover, if a fugitive was tried and found guilty of homicide, the elders of the city to which he had fled were obligated to turn him over to the avenger for execution (Deut. 19:11–13).

D. Involvement of the assembly. Numbers 35:24–25 indicates three ways in which "the congregation"—a selected assembly of Levites—would become involved in the life of the individual who had fled to their city. First, the congregation would " ' "judge between the slayer and the blood avenger" ' " according to the biblical criteria for murder and manslaughter (v. 24; cf. vv. 16–23). The levitical assembly would take whatever time was necessary to honestly and objectively weigh the evidence regarding the case before them. Second, if the defendant was found innocent, the priests would " ' "deliver [him] from the hand of the blood avenger" ' " (v. 25a). That is, they would protect the fugitive from execution. Finally, the assembly would take steps to " ' "restore [the fugitive] to his city of refuge to which he [had] fled" ' " (v. 25b). With loving care, the Levites would help restore the dignity and worth of the fugitive.

III. Providing Shelter Today: What Is Required?

Now that we know some of what the Hebrews did to provide shelter for people in trouble, we need to ask ourselves what *we* can do. After all, the Lord has not commanded the Church to build cities of refuge. So what can Christians do to help the hurting . . . the wounded . . . the brokenhearted . . . the shipwrecked? The answer is given in a nutshell in 1 John 3:

> We know what love is because Christ laid down his life for us. We must in turn lay down our lives for our brothers. But as for the well-to-do man who sees his brother in want but shuts his heart against him, how could anyone believe that the love of God lives in him? My children, let us love not merely in theory or in words—let us love in sincerity and in practice![5] (vv. 16–18)

In other words, *we are to be people of refuge.* If we take this truth seriously, its implementation will involve our commitment to develop these four things:

---

4. See Eugene H. Merrill's commentary, "Numbers," in *The Bible Knowledge Commentary: Old Testament Edition,* eds. John F. Walvoord and Roy B. Zuck (Wheaton, Ill.: Victor Books, 1985), p. 257.

5. J. B. Phillips, *The New Testament in Modern English,* rev. ed. (New York: The Macmillan Co., 1972), p. 504.

A. **A willingness to go the distance for someone in trouble.**
B. **An attitude of loving compassion for those in need.**
C. **An availability to assist people in practical, tangible ways.**
D. **A concern to help others feel needed and important in an increasingly impersonal society.**

Living Insights

This lesson likened the ancient cities of refuge to our churches and our personal lives. Is your church a place of refuge? Are you?

- Reread Joshua 20, jotting down your observations on the function of the cities of refuge. Follow this by writing your thoughts on this topic as it relates to your church and yourself.

Places and People of Refuge: Then and Now		
Ancient Cities of Refuge	My Church as a Place of Refuge	Myself as a Person of Refuge

🐾 Living Insights

After having studied the cities of refuge, it is possible that you find yourself heaving a sigh and wishing these cities were still in operation. It seems that our society is overrun with isolation and loneliness. Of course, we can begin to change that by becoming people of refuge. Let's use the following questions to help ourselves meet this challenge.

- What are some specific steps you can take this week to reach out to a hurting friend and seek to satisfy his or her need for shelter and hope?

- Since cities of refuge no longer exist, where can the troubled people in your town turn for relief, affirmation, and recovery? Have you ever given thought to starting a ministry that reaches out to people in need—such as alcoholics, divorcées, victims of abuse, retarded people and their parents, senior citizens, or single parents? Would you be willing to pray that God would use you to initiate such a ministry for those who attend your church or live in your community?

Some Things Have Gotta Go!

Joshua 23, Judges 1

Flowers need special care and the right kind of soil in order to flourish. They also require protection from the numerous enemies that can thwart their growth—small creatures, various diseases, and even careless people. Similarly, human relationships cannot become healthy and meaningful without the right kind of environment and the proper protection from outside foes. This is especially true within the family of God. Local churches need to be like spiritual greenhouses—providing the vigorous atmosphere of *relational openness,* the rich soil of *encouragement and compassion,* the nutritious food of *sound doctrine,* and the protective walls of *godly obedience* necessary for Christian growth. Sometimes, however, even the best of greenhouses are attacked by internal or external forces that threaten the plants within. When this happens, the appropriate means of extermination need to be initiated in order to shield the greenery from harm. Likewise, there will come times when the spiritual growth of local congregations will be threatened or hampered by foes of godliness. And once those enemies are identified, they need to have their power or presence removed. For churches cannot become or stay healthy while allowing sin to go unchecked in their midst. We must face the fact that there are occasions when some things have got to go. In this lesson we want to consider what several of those things are so that we can begin to eradicate them from our lives and churches.

I. Growth: The Necessity of the Essentials

First Corinthians 12 provides an excellent analogy for understanding the importance of spiritual growth and unity to the health of the Church and its members. In this chapter the Apostle Paul compares the Church to a human body:

> For even as the body is one and yet has many members, and all the members of the body, though they are many, are one body, so also is Christ. For by one Spirit we were all baptized into one body, whether Jews or Greeks, whether slaves or free, and we were all made to drink of one Spirit. For the body is not one member, but many. If the foot should say, "Because I am not a hand, I am not a part of the body," it is not for this reason any the less a part of the body. And if the ear should say, "Because I am not an eye, I am not a part of the body," it is not for this reason any the less a part of the body. If the whole body were an eye, where would the hearing be? If the whole were hearing, where would the sense of smell be? But now God has placed the members, each one of them, in the body, just as He desired. (vv. 12–18)

Because the individuals who compose Christ's spiritual Body are dependent on each other for the proper functioning of the Body, they need to strive for unity as they grow up in Christ (vv. 25–26, Eph. 4:11–16). But what would happen if some members chose to declare independence—in effect, mutinied and went their own way? Physician Paul Brand answers this by drawing on his knowledge of what occurs when cells "choose to live in the [human] body, sharing its benefits while maintaining complete independence."[1] He writes:

> Sometimes a dreaded thing occurs in the body—a mutiny—resulting in a tumor lipoma.... A lipoma is a low-grade, benign tumor. It derives from a single fat cell, skilled in its lazy role of storing fat, that rebels against the leadership of the body and refuses to give up its reserves. It accepts deposits but ignores withdrawal slips. As that cell multiplies, daughter cells follow its lead and a tumor grows like a fungus, filling in crevices, pressing against muscles and organs. Occasionally a lipoma crowds a vital organ like the eye, pushing it out of alignment or pinching a sensitive nerve, and surgery is required....
>
> A tumor is called benign if its effect is fairly localized and it stays within membrane boundaries. But the most traumatizing condition in the body occurs when disloyal cells defy inhibition. They multiply without any checks on growth, spreading rapidly throughout the body, choking out normal cells. White cells, armed against foreign invaders, will not attack the body's own mutinous cells. Physicians fear no other malfunction more deeply: it is called cancer. For still mysterious reasons, these cells—and they may be cells from the brain, liver, kidney, bone, blood, skin, or other tissues—grow wild, out of control. Each is a healthy, functioning cell, but disloyal, no longer acting in regard for the rest of the body.
>
> Even the white cells, the dependable palace guard, can destroy the body through rebellion. Sometimes they recklessly reproduce, clogging the bloodstream, overloading the lymph system, strangling the body's normal functions—such is leukemia.[2]

As cells are to the human body, so believers are to Christ's spiritual Body. The health of the local church as well as the universal Church is intimately linked with the spiritual vitality of Christians. As long

---

1. Dr. Paul Brand and Philip Yancey, *Fearfully and Wonderfully Made* (Grand Rapids, Mich.: Zondervan Publishing House, 1980), p. 20.

2. Brand and Yancey, *Wonderfully Made,* pp. 59–60.

as believers receive the right spiritual nutrition and exercise and continue to function as God has designed them to, the Body of Christ and its members will remain in good health. However, if Christians rebel against the Lord or fail to partake of the essentials of spiritual growth, they will become like cancerous cells in the human body, strangling the life out of other believers, thereby bringing harm to the Church as well as to themselves.

II. Obedience: The Key to National Preservation

Turning back to the Old Testament, we find a story that yields another helpful analogy of spiritual fitness. The story revolves around the Israelites and their takeover of Canaan. The Hebrews conquered Canaan under the leadership of Joshua. But before they settled down in this fertile land, their aged commander delivered a farewell address that highlighted their need to remain obedient to God. Indeed, if the people failed to stay loyal to the Lord, their very survival as a nation would be threatened. Let's consider what Joshua said.

A. **A review of God's faithfulness.** Joshua opened his second to last speech by recalling how God had faithfully assisted the Hebrews in their military conquest of Canaan (Josh. 23:3). Because the Lord had not failed them, the Israelites were able to have the land apportioned among them " 'as an inheritance for [their] tribes' " (v. 4a). How moved and grateful the Hebrews must have been as they looked over the Promised Land and realized that it was now theirs!

B. **Some commands to God's people.** Lest the Israelites become complacent in their new country, Joshua reminded them that there were pockets of Canaanites which still needed to be removed from the land. He added that the Lord would drive the enemy away as the Hebrews sought to keep the Mosaic Law out of their love for God (vv. 5–6, 8–11). In addition, he gave the Israelites several commands concerning their relationship to the heathen yet residing in Canaan: " 'You may not associate with these nations, these which remain among you, or mention the name of their gods, or make anyone swear by them, or serve them, or bow down to them' " (v. 7). To sum it up, Joshua called on the people to remain distinctively the Lord's, bearing His name and doing His bidding. This required that they completely refuse to adopt the Canaanite lifestyle or permit its presence in the Promised Land.

C. **A warning from God's heart.** What would happen if the Israelites failed to keep Joshua's directives and mingled with the Canaanites? The answer is given in the form of a warning:

"For if you ever go back and cling to the rest of these
nations, these which remain among you, and inter-
marry with them, so that you associate with them
and they with you, know with certainty that the Lord
your God will not continue to drive these nations out
from before you; but they shall be a snare and a trap
to you, and a whip on your sides and thorns in your
eyes, until you perish from off this good land which
the Lord your God has given you." (vv. 12–13)

The Hebrews' disobedience would lead to their demise as a
nation. The people would not only lose God's support, but they
would also suffer at the hands of the Canaanites. The ungodly
inhabitants would become " 'a snare and a trap' " to them by
subtly luring them into a pagan lifestyle. The Canaanites would
also become like " 'whips' " to the Hebrews by forcing them to
submit to an alien will. Moreover, the influence of the Canaanites
would eventually be like " 'thorns' " in the Israelites' eyes, blind-
ing them to what was right in God's sight. No wonder Joshua
commanded the Hebrews to eradicate the Canaanites and their
lifestyle from the land. The spiritual growth and physical survival of God's people hinged on their obedience to the Lord in
this matter.

D. A farewell coupled with a reminder. Knowing that his
time had come, Joshua said good-bye to the people, then reminded them of their experience of God's faithfulness and of
what would happen to them if they transgressed the covenant
God had made with them (vv. 14–16).

III. Consequences: An Account of Human Failure

After Joshua's death (24:29–30), the Hebrews began the "mop up
operation" they had been commanded to perform. Unfortunately,
they did not carry it out completely, but settled for a compromise
that set their eventual downfall in motion. Tribe after tribe allowed
a number of Canaanites to remain in the land (Judg. 1:19–33). And
in one instance, the Hebrew tribe of Dan was actually forced from
their territory by the Amorites, a Canaanite tribe (v. 34). Rather than
obeying God and removing the cancer of paganism from the
Promised Land, the Israelites settled down and "lived among the
Canaanites, the Hittites, the Amorites, the Perizzites, the Hivites, and
the Jebusites; and they took their daughters for themselves as wives,
and gave their own daughters to their sons, and served their gods"
(3:5–6). Consequently, the Lord disciplined His people by causing
them to come under the rule of a heathen, Mesopotamian king for
eight years (v. 8). How tragic! The Hebrews had been set free from
Egypt by God's grace and had been led to Canaan to live as recipients

and stewards of God's abundant riches. But because of their disobedience, the land of plenty they had inherited became an oppressive prison of pain (cf. vv. 11–14).

IV. Removal: Hope for Open Relationships

We have been reminded that the human body cannot stay healthy without the cooperation of its members and the removal of disease from its boundaries, and we have seen that the Israelites could not remain nationally and spiritually strong without obeying the Lord and removing the Canaanite lifestyle from their land. In the same way, the Body of Christ cannot mature in godliness without its members submitting to the Lord and ridding their lives of those spiritual diseases that destroy their Christian vitality. We must, in the power God gives us through His Holy Spirit, remove whatever hinders our relationships with fellow believers and the Lord. So let's get a clear idea of what these hindrances are, for once we identify them, we can take the necessary steps to purge them from our lives and protect ourselves from their destructive influence.

A. **Snares and traps have gotta go.** There are many subtle dangers we need to avoid if we are going to encourage and nourish unguarded relationships and spiritual maturity. Here is a list of some of the more common ones: a judgmental spirit, an unforgiving attitude, suspicion, prejudice, pride, cynicism, and unapproachability. These things cannot gain a foothold in relationships without causing some destruction. Therefore, we must guard ourselves against them and, if they are already present, seek to rid ourselves of them.

B. **Whips have gotta go.** Some threats to Christian growth and healthy relationships are like stinging whips. For example, people can be beaten down by being pressured to meet demands and requirements they are presently unable to fulfill. Also, individuals can become frustrated and ridden with false guilt when an unobtainable model of spiritual maturity is held up before them. Our goal as believers is not to whip people into submitting to a set of rigid rules or force them to pattern their lives after unrealistic models. Rather, the Lord calls on us to compassionately encourage and equip His people to live Christ-centered lives (Eph. 4:11–16, Heb. 10:24–25).

C. **Thorns have gotta go.** Those things that blind us to our spiritual needs are thorns which are borne out of our own persistent rebellion against God. Instead of owning up to our sin and confessing it before the Lord, we try to justify our wrongs, which creates only spiritual blindness. We may even go so far as to parade our evil before others and attempt to get naive and impressionable individuals to adopt our wicked life-style. The Lord will not tolerate this kind of defiance against Him. He will severely deal with it, even to the point of taking our lives (Rom. 1:21–32, 1 Cor. 11:27–34). Therefore, we dare not test the Lord's grace by harboring or promoting sin. Instead, we should confess our sins and strive to live in obedience to God (1 Pet. 1:13–16, 1 John 1:9).

Living Insights

Study One ▬▬▬▬▬▬▬▬▬▬▬▬▬▬▬▬▬▬▬▬▬▬▬▬▬▬▬▬

In Joshua 23, we read the beginning of Joshua's farewell address. Such speeches are usually characterized by depth—in both content and emotion. Let's take a closer look at this one.

- After copying this chart into your notebook, read through Joshua 23:1–16. In the center column jot down the key words of each verse. Then summarize the key concepts of each verse in the right-hand column.

Joshua's Farewell Address—Joshua 23:1–16		
Verses	Key Words	Key Concepts
1		
2		
3		
4		
5		
6		
7		
8		
9		
10		
11		
12		
13		
14		
15		
16		

Continued on next page

Living Insights

Snares, traps, whips, and thorns—these are the things that have gotta go! Were you able to relate to some of the specifics mentioned under the different topics?

- Name some snares, traps, whips, or thorns in your life. Write down at least one, but not more than three or four.
- How can you escape these enslaving elements in your life? Write down a particular strategy you can use to rid your life of these "germs."
- Spend some time asking God to help you with these matters.

Choose for Yourself

Joshua 24

A common opinion among many evangelical Christians today is that the church is only a teaching center . . . a dispenser of information . . . a place where people are fed the truth. Is this viewpoint correct? Let's see. Suppose someone were to ask you, "How is your family?" How would you respond? Would you say, "My family is doing very well; in fact, we are becoming an even better family because we regularly eat sumptuous meals together"? If you were to answer this way, the inquirer would probably think you had either misunderstood the question or did not know what constitutes a healthy, vibrant family. For, as we all know, nutritious food alone does not make a family unit strong. Among other things, open and affirming relationships constitute a maturing family. What is true of natural families is also true of spiritual families. Local churches are unhealthy if they are only Bible schools. In order to become spiritually strong, congregations need to couple biblical instruction with the development of unguarded, loving relationships. But neither the study of theology nor the development of relationships can be forced. Each church—indeed, each individual—must freely decide to grow deeper in faith and fellowship. The fact that these are matters of choice is brought out in the last chapter of Joshua. Let's zero in on this passage, bearing in mind what choices *we* need to make concerning our vertical and horizontal relationships.

I. Decisions That Encourage Relationships

In the previous lesson we examined the first farewell address Joshua gave the Hebrews. In this study we will consider the last one he delivered prior to the Israelites' attempt to take complete possession of Canaan.

A. The major factor. After reviewing for the Hebrews what God had done for them from the time of Abraham to the conquest of Canaan (Josh. 24:1–13), Joshua called on the people to make a decision for themselves—one that would make or break their national and spiritual future:

> "Now, therefore, fear the Lord and serve Him in sincerity and truth; and put away the gods which your fathers served beyond the River and in Egypt, and serve the Lord. And if it is disagreeable in your sight to serve the Lord, choose for yourselves today whom you will serve: whether the gods which your fathers served which were beyond the River, or the gods of the Amorites in whose land you are living; but as for me and my house, we will serve the Lord." (vv. 14–15)

Joshua's exhortation confirms that godliness cannot be demanded any more than love can be forced. Forced love is a shotgun wedding, not true love, and legislated godliness is slavery, not genuine righteousness. The road to spiritual maturity begins with a free personal choice. And the motivation to make the right choice comes best from gentle persuasion rather than verbal demands and threats. Thus, just as Joshua lovingly encouraged the Israelites to choose the right option, so we need to compassionately motivate others to take the path that honors God.

B. Three essential elements. With the choice between serving the true God or false gods laid out before them, the Hebrews made their decision. Choosing to follow Joshua's example, they declared, " 'We also will serve the Lord' " (v. 18b). The text reveals three key parts of their decision.

    1. Fear of the Lord. By acknowledging God as their Master, the Israelites were agreeing with Joshua that they should revere God to the utmost (v. 14a).

    2. Service to the Lord. Three times the Hebrews expressed their unequivocal commitment to become faithful servants of God (vv. 18, 21, 24).

    3. Obedience to the Lord. They also declared their intention to heed God's counsel (v. 24b).

C. The ultimate benefit. When the Israelites aligned their choice with God's revealed will, they received the Lord's faithful support and abundant favor. Of course, as we saw in our previous study, the Hebrews eventually compromised their commitment to God (Judg. 1–3). But even so, the Lord remained devoted to them, always acting in their best interest, whether it was through discipline, deliverance, or development (see Judg. 3–9).

II. What Is Your Choice?

When it comes to developing vulnerable, caring relationships, there is one major factor that overshadows all the rest: *We cannot be rightly related to others until we are rightly related to God.* And the Bible makes it clear that the *only* way to God is by faith in His Son, Jesus Christ (John 14:6, Acts 4:10–12, 1 Tim. 2:5–6). When we hear Christ's counsel and act on it, we become like a wise man who builds his home on solid rock—able to withstand the storms of life (Matt. 7:24–25). However, when we listen to the Lord but fail to conform our lives to His Word, we become like a foolish man who constructs his house on shifting sand—unprepared to handle the crises of life (vv. 26–27). Therefore, whether we stand or fall, grow or wither, relate deeply or superficially, all depends on what decision we make concerning our relationship to Christ. And regarding that choice, there are only three ways each of us can go. *We can choose to commit ourselves to Him,* which is the only option that can bring earthly contentment and heavenly bliss. Or *we can choose to reject Him*—a choice that has nothing to offer but death. Or *we can choose to delay our decision to accept or reject Him.* But this choice is really rejection in disguise, for the only way to be freed from sin and its consequences is to trust in the Savior. And that requires a decision to cling to Him—a decision that "fence straddling" does not allow. So what will it be? Will you choose Christ, and thereby embark on the road to more meaningful relationships? Or will you turn your back on Him, and thereby deprive yourself of the ability to enjoy others to the fullest? The choice is yours to make. No one can make it for you.

💈 *Living Insights*

Study One ▬▬▬▬▬▬▬▬▬▬▬▬▬▬▬▬▬▬▬▬▬▬▬▬▬▬▬▬▬▬

The central passage in this study is Joshua 24:14–15. This pair of verses may be familiar to you, but let's use them in a way that will produce long-range results in our lives.

- Let's *memorize* Joshua 24:14–15. Write the verses out on an index card and read them aloud slowly, eight or ten times. Then try writing them out several times. This process will help you treasure God's Word in your heart so that you will not stray from the truth (Ps. 119:11).

💈 *Living Insights*

Study Two ▬▬▬▬▬▬▬▬▬▬▬▬▬▬▬▬▬▬▬▬▬▬▬▬▬▬▬▬▬▬

We are what we are largely because of our individual choices. Let's come to terms with this fact.

- Reflect on an area in your life that consistently gives you trouble— trouble caused by your own choices. As you analyze this struggle, consider the relationship between your bad choices and their consequences. Would you like to change this situation? You can by beginning to replace the wrong choices with the right ones. This process may include coming before God and seeking counsel from His Word and mature Christian friends. Whatever it takes, don't put off your need to change any longer. Confront it head-on in the power of God's Spirit (Rom. 6–8).

The Necessity of Accountability
Selected Scripture

When we buy something on credit or secure a loan, we are legally responsible to pay our debt; that is, we are financially accountable. We become occupationally accountable when we agree to perform a job under certain contractual terms and regulations. During some periods of our lives, we may even be held accountable academically—when we enroll in a college and decide on a curriculum that requires the satisfactory completion of homework and exams. But what about in the areas of our Christian growth . . . our fellowship with believers . . . our relationship to God? Should we be held accountable in matters such as these? For one reason or another, many of us resist answering yes to this question. For some of us, accountability in the Christian life may smack of legalism; we may view this idea as a violation of our freedom in Christ. It's certainly true that our individualistic, live-and-let-live society snubs the concept of relational accountability. This attitude of independence may have influenced us to reject the idea in the spiritual realm. Whatever the case, we must come to realize that accountability is essential to individual and corporate maturity in the Christian life. So let's zero in on *spiritual accountability* and explore some practical steps we can take to implement it into our lives.

I. Accountability Explained

Before continuing, we need to understand what accountability is, what it requires, and what can happen when it is abused or ignored.

A. A nontechnical definition. For our purposes, being accountable refers to the *willingness to explain and take responsibility for one's actions with an open and nondefensive spirit.* In other words, accountability concerns our motives—the whys of our acts—and our answerability—the responsibility we are willing to accept for our acts.

B. Some necessary character traits. Accountability cannot become a reality in the lives of those who are satisfied with mediocrity. Indeed, the development of accountability in a person's life requires that one seek to rise above the average by becoming vulnerable, teachable, honest, and available.

C. Extremes to avoid. Like any good thing, accountability can be abused or ignored. An example of the first extreme is found in 3 John. Here we are told about a man name Diotrephes—an oppressive, judgmental leader in a first-century church. Notice what the Apostle John said about him:

> I wrote something to the church; but Diotrephes, who loves to be first among them, does not accept what we say. For this reason, if I come, I will call attention to his deeds which he does, unjustly accusing us

with wicked words; and not satisfied with this, neither does he himself receive the brethren, and he forbids those who desire to do so, and puts them out of the church. Beloved, do not imitate what is evil, but what is good. The one who does good is of God; the one who does evil has not seen God. (vv. 9–11)

Diotrephes was determined to hold Christians responsible for adhering to his own set of narrow-minded, pharisaic rules. As a result, he tore believers down, rather than building them up, in their faith. John rightfully stood against this individual's manipulative and destructive use of accountability. The second extreme of accountability was exemplified in the early Corinthian church. This congregation not only overlooked a heinous sin among one of its members, but eventually took pride in the fact that it was allowing evil to go unchecked (1 Cor. 5:1–2). The Apostle Paul appropriately condemned this church and commanded it to discipline the wayward believer for his sin (vv. 3–13). As we seek to understand and implement accountability in our personal lives and local assemblies, we need to watch out for these extremes so that we do not fall prey to them. For either one can ruin a church and destroy healthy relationships.

II. Accountability in Scripture

Now that we know what accountability is, we are ready to turn to the Scriptures for its support. With even a cursory survey of the biblical record, we will see that God backs both vertical and horizontal accountability, and that with the practice of accountability come some significant benefits.

A. Accountability to God. Several scriptural texts speak of our accountability to the Lord. For example, in Matthew 12 Jesus says, " 'I say to you, that every careless word that men shall speak, they shall render account for it in the day of judgment' " (v. 36). The Apostle Paul reiterates this with ringing clarity: "We shall all stand before the judgment seat of God. For it is written, 'As I live, says the Lord, every knee shall bow to Me, / And every tongue shall give praise to God.' So then each one of us shall give account of himself to God" (Rom. 14:10b–12; cf. 1 Pet. 4:4–5).

B. Accountability to man. We are not only responsible to God, but also to one another. For instance, we are accountable to our church leaders (Heb. 13:17) and our governmental authorities (Rom. 13:1–7). We are also duty-bound to serve and devote ourselves to all fellow Christians in love (12:9–10, 13, 17; 15:1–2). The Scriptures further obligate us to gently confront and restore those Christians who have fallen into sin (Gal. 6:1–2,

James 5:19–20). In fact, we are even held responsible for confessing our wrongs to one another (James 5:16). The bottom line is that God knows we need each other—if for no other reason than to help keep one another from straying from the path of righteousness.

C. Two benefits of accountability. Although the Bible gives numerous benefits of accountability, here we will concentrate our thoughts on two of them.

    1. By being accountable, we are less likely to stumble into traps. We all have blind spots—areas in our lives that we do not see as personal hazards or moral inconsistencies. So we need the wise counsel—even reproofs—of others to help guard us from becoming victims of our own blindness. Several passages in Proverbs bring this truth out:

> Through presumption comes nothing but strife,
> But with those who receive counsel is wisdom.
> (13:10)
> The teaching of the wise is a fountain of life,
> To turn aside from the snares of death. (v. 14)
> Poverty and shame will come to him who neglects discipline,
> But he who regards reproof will be honored. (v. 18)
> He who neglects discipline despises himself,
> But he who listens to reproof acquires understanding. (15:32)
> Oil and perfume make the heart glad,
> So a man's counsel is sweet to his friend. (27:9)
> Iron sharpens iron,
> So one man sharpens another. (v. 17)

    2. By being accountable, we don't get away with unwise and sinful actions. Not one of us is without sin (Rom. 3:9–18, 23). And not one of us succeeds in our every battle against sin. Indeed, most of us occasionally engage in activities that we know are wrong, but that we are still unwilling to give up. Therefore, we need to have people in our lives who are unafraid to lovingly confront us when we go astray. The Apostle Peter had the Apostle Paul, who rebuked him in public for contradicting the very heart of the gospel—salvation by faith apart from works (Gal. 2:11–21). King Saul had the prophet Samuel, who confronted him about his violation of God's command to completely destroy the Amalekites (1 Sam. 15:10–23). And King David had the prophet Nathan, who exposed his sins of adultery, murder, and deceit (2 Sam. 12:1–14). As embarrassing and painful as confrontations might be, we desperately need them. For, as one proverb states, "Stripes that wound scour away evil, / And strokes reach the innermost parts" (Prov. 20:30). Without "the wounds of a friend," at best, all we have left are the "deceitful . . . kisses of an enemy" (27:6).

III. Accountability Applied

There is no doubt about it—accountability is absolutely necessary and tremendously beneficial to our individual and corporate growth in Christ. Given this, it is important that we make accountability a part of our lives. Here are four practical suggestions that can help us do this.

A. Stop and consider the value of becoming accountable.

B. Ask yourself three questions: Do I tend to remain isolated and unaccountable? If so, why? What will happen if I stay in this condition?

C. Choose at least one godly person with whom you can meet regularly and relate to deeply.

D. Develop some relationships that will strengthen your grip on spiritual things.

Continued on next page

🔥 *Living Insights*

This lesson has shown us that the Bible has much to say in support of spiritual accountability. Let's look at several of the relevant passages more closely.

- The chart below records various biblical texts that speak to the matter of accountability. Study each passage and summarize their teaching on this topic.

Accountability in Scripture			
Verses	Summaries	Verses	Summaries
Proverbs 13:10		Romans 12:8–10	
13:14		13:1–7	
13:18		14:10b–12	
13:20		15:14	
15:31		1 Corinthians 5:1–13	
15:32		2 Corinthians 5:10	
20:30		Galatians 5:25–6:2	
27:6		Hebrews 13:16–17	
27:9		James 5:16, 19–20	
27:17		1 Peter 4:4–5	
Matthew 12:36		3 John 9–11	

🔥 *Living Insights*

Are you accountable? Not just at work, but in your personal life? If you aren't, you face some tough questions: Why do I remain unaccountable? What will happen if I stay in this condition?

- If you are personally accountable to someone, use this opportunity to pray for that person. If you are not, take time to look back over this lesson. Do whatever you must to begin a relationship of account-ability. This is not an area of your life in which you can cut corners. Find a person to whom you can be accountable—don't delay!

A Hope Transplant:
The Essential Operation
Proverbs 13:12, 1 Peter 5:1–10

Churches are like children. They come in different shapes and sizes, with different bents and personalities. No two congregations are exactly alike. But whether a church is large or small, emotional or stoic, liberal or conservative, missions-minded or instruction-centered, loosely structured or tightly led, the one essential it must have to maintain vibrancy and effectiveness is *hope*. Take hope away and you suck the lifeblood out of a church. Indeed, hope is one of the necessary ingredients in turning an uptight congregation into an unguarded one. But what exactly is hope? Is it really all that essential? How can it be reborn and nurtured in a church? These are the questions we will concern ourselves with here.

I. The Meaning and Necessity of Hope
Let's turn our attention first to what hope is and why it is so important.

A. The biblical definition. The various Greek words for *hope* in the New Testament "never indicate a vague or a fearful antici-pation, but always the expectation of something good."[1] Fur-thermore, biblical hope is always confident and centered on the Lord.[2] Given these understandings, we can define *hope* as "the confident expectation of receiving something good from God."

B. Our need for biblical hope. Do we need this kind of hope? Can we live without it? On the surface, it seems that human beings can function without biblical hope. After all, there are many people in the world who do not believe in any sort of deity and yet seem to do just fine in life. But when we look more closely at the lives of many atheists, we soon discover that if they have hope,[3] it is usually based on an unfounded optimism in the progress of man through education, technology, and

The cassette message that corresponds to this chapter was formerly titled "Churches of Hope."

1. E. Hoffmann, "Hope, Expectation," in *The New International Dictionary of New Testament Theology*, 3 vols. (Grand Rapids, Mich.: Zondervan Publishing House, 1975, 1976, 1978), vol. 2, p. 241.

2. See Hoffmann, "Hope, Expectation," pp. 242–43.

3. At least two kinds of atheists deny that man can have any real hope. Atheistic nihilists believe that life is completely void of value, purpose, or meaning. Atheistic existentialists agree with the nihilists on that point, but they go on to assert that individuals should revolt against the absurdity of life and create their own value, hope, and meaning. Some books that further explain and evaluate these viewpoints are: *The Universe Next Door: A Basic World View Catalog,* by James W. Sire (Downers Grove, Ill.: InterVarsity Press, 1976); *Existentialism: The Philosophy of Despair and the Quest for Hope,* by C. Stephen Evans (Grand Rapids, Mich.: Zondervan Publishing House; Dallas: Probe Ministries International, 1984); *The Dust of Death,* by Os Guinness (Downers Grove, Ill.: InterVarsity Press, 1973).

science. An excellent example of this type of thinking is found in the *Humanist Manifesto II:*

> The next century can be and should be the humanistic century.... We have virtually conquered the planet, explored the moon, overcome the natural limits of travel and communication; we stand at the dawn of a new age, ready to move farther into space and perhaps inhabit other planets. Using technology wisely, we can control our environment, conquer poverty, markedly reduce disease, extend our life-span, significantly modify our behavior, alter the course of human evolution and cultural develop-ment, unlock vast new powers, and provide human-kind with unparalleled opportunity for achieving an abundant and meaningful life.[4]

Is this faith in man's ability warranted? Ironically, atheistic hu-manist David Ehrenfeld thinks not. In a scathing critique of secular humanism, he writes these penetrating words against the humanistic hope in man:

> The major reason for the prevalence of [expressions like] *hopefully = let us hope* is that deep within our-selves we know that our omnipotence is a sham, our knowledge and control of the future is weak and limited, our inventions and discoveries work, if they work at all, in ways that we do not expect, our plan-ning is meaningless, our systems are running amok—in short, that the humanistic assumptions upon which our societies are grounded lack validity. We are trying to fool ourselves, and although we keep on trying we know it nonetheless. Evidence is piled all around us that the religion of [humanism] is self-destructive and foolish, yet the more it fails the more arrogant and preposterous are the claims of its priests.[5]

For man to hope in himself is not only useless and misguided but deceptive. In fact, it is to fall victim to the oldest con in human history—the lie that man is God and therefore can save himself. Ehrenfeld expresses it this way:

> We have been reading the old biblical story of the expulsion from the Garden of Eden too carelessly of late; like fundamentalists, we must pay more attention

---

4. *Humanist Manifestos I and II,* ed. Paul Kurtz (Buffalo, N.Y.: Prometheus Books, 1973), p. 14.

5. David Ehrenfeld, *The Arrogance of Humanism* (New York: Oxford University Press, 1978), p. 58.

to detail. For was not the Garden of Eden described as a *better* place than the world outside after the fall? And was it not the clear implication of Genesis that all the new-found skills and knowledge that the fateful apple could provide were imperfect? The serpent was lying when he said, "Ye shall be as gods."[6]

Therefore, true hope—the kind that gives real meaning and purpose to life—is biblical hope. And the Scriptures make it clear that we need this hope. Notice what Proverbs 13:12 says about it: "Hope deferred makes the heart sick, / But desire fulfilled is a tree of life." The Hebrew word for *sick* conveys the idea of being diseased. When the term is used in reference to nations, it refers to calamity, grief, or affliction. In other words, when hope is unfulfilled, the heart is stricken with sorrow and pain. Or, as one paraphrase renders the thought, "When hope is crushed, the heart is crushed."[7] People usually do not live long with dashed hopes. And neither do churches.

II. Some Ways to Keep Hope Strong

So how can we keep the disease of hopelessness away from our churches? What does it take to foster and maintain hope in congregations? The answers are embedded in 1 Peter 5:1–10. Here the Apostle Peter offers five pieces of counsel that, if followed, can restore and preserve genuine hope.

A. Provide the right kind of leadership. Writing to Christians who were suffering intense persecution, Peter encouraged his readers to press on in their faith individually and collectively. But he never pulled rank on them by lording his apostolic authority over them. Instead, he referred to himself as a fellow believer (1 Pet. 1:3) and "fellow elder" (5:1a) in his letter to these hurting Christians. From this humble standpoint, Peter exhorted them to "shepherd the flock of God" (v. 2a). We must understand that the ministry of shepherding is broader than that of preaching and teaching. It includes leadership, care, protection, commitment, and acceptance. The nature of the task implies that congregations need these qualities in their leaders in order to grow as they should. Put another way, uptight, superdefensive, unloving leaders will not produce churches characterized by close, compassionate, loving relationships. Furthermore, shepherding is to be done willingly, enthusiastically, and exemplarily. Individuals are not to be pushed into leadership positions. Nor should people become leaders for

---

6. Ehrenfeld, *Arrogance,* pp. 124–25.

7. *Good News Bible,* American Bible Society, 1976.

money or power (vv. 2–3). These contrasting qualifications point to an enemy of good church leadership—*faulty models.* Few things will crush a congregation's hope as quickly as a leader who is "shepherding" for the wrong reasons and with the wrong attitudes. Churches need to pick their shepherds carefully, making sure that their candidates meet the biblical criteria for church leaders (1 Tim. 3:1–13, Titus 1:5–9).[8]

B. Be truly humble toward one another. This bit of counsel is conveyed in these words: "You younger men, likewise, be subject to your elders; and *all of you,* clothe yourselves with humility toward one another, for God is opposed to the proud, but gives grace to the humble. Humble yourselves, therefore, under the mighty hand of God, that He may exalt you at the proper time" (1 Pet. 5:5–6, emphasis added). As this passage indicates, the opposite of humility is *pride.* Humility exalts others; pride exalts self. Humility serves others; pride serves self. Humility bows before God; pride bows before self. Humble people share, remain teachable, and care about others; prideful people hoard, are closed-minded, and use others to achieve their own selfish ends. No wonder the God of grace and self-giving love hates pride! If we want our churches to flourish, we need to put on humility and strip ourselves of pride (cf. Phil. 2:1–11).

C. Release anxiety. In addition, we need to cast our worries onto God (1 Pet. 5:7). Because He loves us, we can trust Him to meet our needs and to replace our worries with peaceful assurance (Matt. 6:25–34, 11:28–30; John 14:1, 27). However, if we choose to hold on to our anxious concerns, we will become weary and dull. A worry-laden church loses its cutting edge and retreats from new challenges. Without releasing its burden, it will suffocate and collapse under the oppressive weight.

D. Have an alert and discerning awareness of the enemy. The Apostle Peter put it this way: "Be of sober spirit, be on the alert. Your adversary, the devil, prowls about like a roaring lion, seeking someone to devour. But resist him, firm in your faith, knowing that the same experiences of suffering are being accomplished by your brethren who are in the world" (1 Pet. 5:8–9). It is certainly true that many Christians see Satan behind every nook and cranny. Anything that goes sour, they attribute to him. Some believers have reacted to this viewpoint by not taking Satan seriously at all. Consequently, many of them have become ignorant victims of his schemes. We need to find a balance

---

8. A discussion of the biblical qualifications for church leaders may be found in the study guide titled *Excellence in Ministry,* ed. Bill Watkins, from the Bible-teaching ministry of Charles R. Swindoll (Fullerton, Calif.: Insight for Living, 1985), pp. 39–56.

between these extremes. Because the devil and his cohorts are not omnipotent, omnipresent, or sovereign, we can rest assured that they are not responsible for all the evil in the world. In fact, the Bible lays much of the responsibility for sin on our doorstep (Gen. 3, Rom. 5:12–21, James 1:13–15). On the other hand, since Satan is out to derail Christians from their walk with God, we dare not remain naive of his tactics or face his attacks unprotected. We need to stand firm against our demonic adversary, clothed in the armor of God (Eph. 6:10–18).

E. **Respond well to adversity.** When we suffer, we can either internalize the hurt and feel sorry for ourselves, or turn our eyes toward heaven and ask God to restore us in His way and according to His timetable. Throughout 1 Peter, the second response is held up as the right one (2:18–24, 3:13–18, 4:12–19). Undoubtedly, we will experience hardship during our lives. When we do, we should view it as an opportunity, not a barrier, to spiritual growth. For if we allow our sufferings to overwhelm us, to crush our spirit, we will lose our hope and miss some of the greatest lessons God has to teach us. But if we face them arm in arm with other believers, looking to the Lord for strength to endure, we will grow strong in our faith, both individually and corporately. Philip Yancey makes the point well:

By taking it on Himself, Jesus in a sense dignified pain. Of all the kinds of lives He could have lived, He chose a suffering one. Because of Jesus, I can never say about a person, "He must be suffering because of some sin he committed"; Jesus, who did not sin, also felt pain. And I cannot say, "Suffering and death must mean God has forsaken us; He's left us alone to self-destruct." Because even though Jesus died, His death became the great victory of history, pulling man and God together. God made a supreme good out of that awful day.

Jesus' followers are not insulated from the tragedies of this world, just as He was not. God has never promised that tornados will skip our houses on the way to our pagan neighbors'. Microbes do not flee from Christian bodies. Rather, Peter could say to suffering Christians, "This suffering is all part of the work God has given you. Christ, who suffered for you, is your example. Follow in his steps" (1 Peter 2:21 LB). The Bible goes further, using phrases I will not attempt to explain such as "partakers in His suffering" and "complete His suffering," indicating that suffering can be, not a horror to be shed at all costs, but a means of grace to make us more like God.[9]

III. A Closing Challenge

Have you lost hope? Are you isolating yourself as a result? If so, you are only pushing yourself deeper into despair. The way out of your dark pit involves sharing your pain with God and some believers who can help you. Remember Paul's words: "If one member [of the Body of Christ] suffers, all the members suffer with it" (1 Cor. 12:26a). Give the Lord and His people a chance to share your burden and meet some of your needs. This will require you to be unguarded, which may be uncomfortable at first. But when you consider that the alternative is loneliness and despair, there seems to be no good reason to keep your hurt locked inside. So let it out. Open yourself up. The love of God and of His children awaits you.

---

9. Philip Yancey, *Where Is God When It Hurts?* (Grand Rapids, Mich.: Zondervan Publishing House, 1977), pp. 162–63.

Living Insights

Let's take some time to look back over our study. Have you been sufficiently encouraged to drop your guard? How has this time caused you to loosen your mask?

- The following chart includes the titles of our thirteen studies. Let's use this time to review the most noteworthy truth you learned from each lesson. Jot each one down in the right-hand column.

Dropping Your Guard	
Lesson Titles	Most Noteworthy Truths
Loosening the Mask: How It All Began	
Digging Deeper, Risking Change (Part One)	
Digging Deeper, Risking Change (Part Two)	
Getting Closer, Growing Stronger	
Operation Assimilation	
United and Invincible	
When the Fellowship Breaks Down	
Authentic Love	
Needed: Shelter for Storm Victims	
Some Things Have Gotta Go!	
Choose for Yourself	
The Necessity of Accountability	
A Hope Transplant: The Essential Operation	

Continued on next page

77

Living Insights

Let's continue our review. But this time let's concentrate on application.

- Copy the following chart into your notebook. As you browse through the material we've covered in this study, search out the most significant application you made from each lesson. Record your findings in the right-hand column.

Dropping Your Guard	
Lesson Titles	Most Noteworthy Applications
Loosening the Mask: How It All Began	
Digging Deeper, Risking Change (Part One)	
Digging Deeper, Risking Change (Part Two)	
Getting Closer, Growing Stronger	
Operation Assimilation	
United and Invincible	
When the Fellowship Breaks Down	
Authentic Love	
Needed: Shelter for Storm Victims	
Some Things Have Gotta Go!	
Choose for Yourself	
The Necessity of Accountability	
A Hope Transplant: The Essential Operation	

Acknowledgments

Insight for Living is grateful for permission to quote from the following sources:

Brand, Dr. Paul, and Yancey, Philip. *Fearfully and Wonderfully Made.* Grand Rapids, Mich.: Zondervan Publishing House, 1980.

Ehrenfeld, David. *The Arrogance of Humanism.* New York: Oxford University Press, 1978.

Kurtz, Paul, ed. *Humanist Manifestos I and II.* Buffalo, N.Y.: Prometheus Books, 1973.

Larson, Bruce, and Miller, Keith. *The Edge of Adventure.* Waco, Tex.: Word Books, 1974.

Lewis, C. S. *The Four Loves.* New York: Harcourt Brace Jovanovich; London: William Collins Sons and Co., 1960.

———. *The Problem of Pain.* New York: Macmillan Publishing Co.; London: William Collins Sons and Co., 1962.

Phillips, J. B. *The New Testament in Modern English.* Rev. ed. New York: The Macmillan Co.; London: SCM Press, 1972.

Unger, Merrill F. "Cities of Refuge." In *Unger's Bible Dictionary.* Rev. ed. Chicago: Moody Press, 1966.

Yancey, Philip. *Where Is God When It Hurts?* Grand Rapids, Mich.: Zondervan Publishing House, 1977.

Insight for Living
Cassette Tapes
DROPPING YOUR GUARD

In our mask-wearing, superficial age when surface relationships are much more popular than authentic and meaningful involvement in one another's lives, this series offers a different approach to the life of the church. It is a strong, affirming statement that upholds the value of open, unguarded relationships. Based on those days when the Hebrews were freed from Egyptian bondage and on their way to the land of Canaan, these twelve messages will motivate you to stop skating and start relating!

			U.S.	Canadian
DYG	CS	Cassette series—includes album cover	$34.50	$43.75
		Individual cassettes—include messages A and B	5.00	6.35

These prices are effective as of July 1986 and are subject to change without notice.

DYG 1-A: ***Digging Deeper, Risking Change (Part One)***
Exodus 13, Numbers 11
   B: ***Digging Deeper, Risking Change (Part Two)***
Exodus 13–14, Numbers 11–14

DYG 2-A: ***Getting Closer, Growing Stronger***
Deuteronomy 6, Joshua 1
   B: ***Operation Assimilation***
Joshua 1:1–18

DYG 3-A: ***United and Invincible***
Joshua 1, 6, 8, 10
   B: ***When the Fellowship Breaks Down***
Joshua 7

DYG 4-A: ***Authentic Love***
1 Corinthians 13:1–8a
   B: ***Needed: Shelter for Storm Victims***
Selected Scripture

DYG 5-A: ***Some Things Have Gotta Go!***
Joshua 23, Judges 1
   B: ***Choose for Yourself***
Joshua 24

DYG 6-A: ***The Necessity of Accountability***
Selected Scripture
   B: ***A Hope Transplant: The Essential Operation****
Proverbs 13:12, 1 Peter 5:1–10

*This message was formerly titled "Churches of Hope."

Ordering Information

U.S. ordering information: You are welcome to use our toll-free number (for Visa and MasterCard orders only) between the hours of 8:30 A.M. and 4:00 P.M., Pacific time, Monday through Friday. The number is **(800) 772-8888.** This number may be used anywhere in the continental United States excluding California, Hawaii, and Alaska. Orders from those areas are handled through our Sales Department at **(714) 870-9161.** We are unable to accept collect calls.

Your order will be processed promptly. We ask that you allow four to six weeks for delivery by fourth-class mail. If you wish your order to be shipped first-class, please add 10 percent of the total order cost (not including California sales tax) for shipping and handling.

Canadian ordering information: Your order will be processed promptly. We ask that you allow approximately four weeks for delivery by first-class mail to the U.S./Canadian border. All orders will be shipped from our office in Fullerton, California. For our listeners in British Columbia, a 7 percent sales tax must be added to the total of all tape orders (not including first-class postage). For further information, please contact our office at **(604) 272-5811.**

Payment options: We accept personal checks, money orders, Visa, and MasterCard in payment for materials ordered. Unfortunately, we are unable to offer invoicing or COD orders. If the amount of your check or money order is less than the amount of your purchase, your check will be returned so that you may place your order again with the correct amount. All orders must be paid in full before shipment can be made.

Returned checks: There is a $10 charge for any returned check (regardless of the amount of your order) to cover processing and invoicing.

Guarantee: Our tapes are guaranteed for ninety days against faulty performance or breakage due to a defect in the tape. For best results, please be sure your tape recorder is in good operating condition and is cleaned regularly.

Mail your order to one of the following addresses:

Insight for Living
Sales Department
Post Office Box 4444
Fullerton, CA 92634

Insight for Living Ministries
Post Office Box 2510
Vancouver, BC
Canada V6B 3W7

Quantity discounts and gift certificates are available upon request.

Overseas ordering information is provided on the reverse side of the order form.

Order Form

Please send me the following cassette tapes:

The current series: ☐ DYG CS Dropping Your Guard

Individual cassettes: ☐ DYG 1   ☐ DYG 2   ☐ DYG 3

                              ☐ DYG 4   ☐ DYG 5   ☐ DYG 6

I am enclosing:

$_____   To purchase the cassette series for $34.50 (in Canada $43.75*) which includes the album cover

$_____   To purchase individual tapes at $5.00 each (in Canada $6.35*)

$_____   Total of purchases

$_____   California residents please add 6 percent sales tax

$_____   U.S. residents please add 10 percent for first-class shipping and handling if desired

$_____   *British Columbia residents please add 7 percent sales tax

$_____   Canadian residents please add 6 percent for postage

$_____   **Overseas residents please add appropriate postage** (See postage chart under "Overseas Ordering Information.")

$_____   As a gift to the Insight for Living radio ministry for which a tax-deductible receipt will be issued

$_____   **Total amount due (Please do not send cash.)**

Form of payment:

☐ Check or money order made payable to Insight for Living

☐ Credit card (Visa or MasterCard only)

If there is a balance: ☐ apply it as a donation   ☐ please refund

---

Credit card purchases:

☐ Visa   ☐ MasterCard number _____

Expiration date _____

Signature _____

We cannot process your credit card purchase without your signature.

Name _____

Address _____

_____

City _____

State/Province _____ Zip/Postal code _____

Country _____

Telephone (   ) _____ Radio Station __ __ __ __

Should questions arise concerning your order, we may need to contact you.

Overseas Ordering Information

If you do not live in the United States or Canada, please note the following information. This will ensure efficient processing of your request.

Estimated time of delivery: We ask that you allow approximately twelve to sixteen weeks for delivery by surface mail. If you would like your order sent airmail, the length of delivery may be reduced. All orders will be shipped from our office in Fullerton, California.

Payment options: Due to fluctuating currency rates, we can accept only personal checks made payable in U.S. funds, international money orders, Visa, and MasterCard in payment for materials ordered. If the amount of your check or money order is less than the amount of your purchase, your check will be returned so that you may place your order again with the correct amount. All orders must be paid in full before shipment can be made.

Returned checks: There is a $10 charge for any returned check (regardless of the amount of your order) to cover processing and invoicing.

Postage and handling: Please add to the amount of purchase the basic postage cost for the service you desire. All orders must include postage based on the chart below.

Purchase Amount		Surface Postage	Airmail Postage
From	To	Percentage of Order	Percentage of Order
$ .01	$15.00	40%	75%
15.01	75.00	25%	45%
75.01	or more	15%	40%

Guarantee: Our tapes are guaranteed for ninety days against faulty performance or breakage due to a defect in the tape. For best results, please be sure your tape recorder is in good operating condition and is cleaned regularly.

Mail your order or inquiry to the following address:

Insight for Living
Sales Department
Post Office Box 4444
Fullerton, CA 92634

Quantity discounts and gift certificates are available upon request.